Survival Snapshots:

Defending Home
Against Sex Addiction

Annie Elizabeth Farmer

T0002206

Twin Fawns Press

Names have been varied so that only those who want to acknowledge themselves in this book need do so. To the best of my recollection, everything else is true.

For my mothers, especially Mom

For my daughters

For the alphabet of friends who will find themselves in this book: for their support, encouragement, reading and proofreading

For Clay

Survival Snapshots:
The Picture Album

We are approaching autumn of 2011 as I prepare this book to go out into the world. Although I have been a professional writer for over thirty years, I find myself more tentative about sending this book into the world than anything I have written before. Survival Snapshots: Defending Home Against Sex Addiction is not a book I ever planned to write, even after a divorce six years ago from my husband of twenty-eight years. Certainly, it is not a book I wanted to write. It is a book I had to write.

In late winter of 2010, I remember thinking I was maybe—just maybe—going to survive my divorce of then five years. I had somehow gotten my two daughters through college; I had nursed my elderly mother through a major illness and moved her nearby; I was working steadily again on a novel. At least I still had a home surrounded by nature where I was still able to write, where my children could come home as needed, and where I was able to continue to recover from betrayal from the man I had loved since I was twenty-one-years old, combined with the death of my sister of the heart at the same time.

I had no energy or desire to fight with my ex-husband, whom I am calling Joseph in this book. (All people's names in this book, including my own, have been altered.) I was worn out—physically, emotionally, mentally, financially, and almost spiritually. But on a February afternoon in 2010, I opened the mailbox to find a copy of papers filed by a lawyer I had never heard of, alleging that my former husband had been treated unfairly and was pleading with the judge to change our divorce agreement.

At least on paper, his objective was to force me to sell my final refuge, my home. I have come to believe the real matter was an extension of the cause of our divorce—a sexual addiction that has changed the loving husband I knew into an angry, unhappy man who wanted to blame anyone but himself for his problems. He especially wanted to make me, his wife of twenty-eight years and the mother of his children, pay for how he felt. In short, he will never forgive me for him destroying our life together.

This was on a Thursday and he was asking the judge to consider his plea the next Tuesday. After a weekend of where I remember myself resembling "the mad woman in the attic," I was able to see my divorce lawyer yet again and to begin once again to fight a battle I had never expected, to fight with the man I had so loved who had become an enemy.

As I slogged through the legal system, I lost all energy to write the novel. I was doing well to write a grocery list. Yet another betrayal by the husband I had loved and trusted brought up all of those barely healed emotions that had been caused by his descent into sexual addiction—an addiction that had devastated the marriage and family we had built for so many years. My Dr. Jekyll had drunk a fatal dose of the potion and Mr. Hyde was firmly in charge.

I had survived the divorce itself, but now I found myself too much mentally in a heartbroken place, again. Beyond the legal battle, how was I going to fight the despair that threatened to overwhelm me a second time? I began to think how I had arrived here in this place and so, most mornings before teaching or seeing lawyers or even breakfast, I began to write reflections for myself about what I was experiencing now—and the experiences both lovely and horrible that had preceded this time in my life. I was turning fifty-five years old that spring and decided I'd better find some of that wise woman strength within if I was going to make it to fifty-six in any form of sanity

These reflections from late winter to autumn 2010 constitute the body of this book. The more I wrote, the more I wondered if my experience would help others who were living with the pain of trying to save a relationship where their partner had become an addict, others who had finally had to survive on their own, and perhaps even be a tool to help addicts themselves be more aware of the consequences to their loved ones of such addictions.

I also realized we all have times when we must face survival in life from many things: illness, deaths of family and friends, children leaving home, seeing our parents age, and just growing older ourselves. I offer these reflections of my own survival—thus far—to I hope help others survive.

Survival Snapshots is not meant to be a self-help book in a traditional sense. It is my conversation with you as you look through my picture album of snapshots, showing that I didn't fall off some cliff of despair but climbed back up, glad to be alive, and sometimes by the grace of God even able to laugh!

These reflections are not in strict chronological order, but were written with the mixture of past and present experiences that I found to write about in the morning reflections of those nine months of 2010. To show where I was in the time of the writing and those in the progress of the legal battle, I have noted the season (late winter, spring, summer, midsummer, approaching fall) at the top of each snapshot. Think of photographs you look through with their penciled dates that capture the moments that led up to that snapshot and might predict the future of the impact of that moment on the rest of life.

Late Winter, 2010
Survival Snapshot: Hawk, Home, Monster

This year again, a pair of red-tailed hawks have nested somewhere in my oak, hickory and hackberry woods. Since late January they have been circling in wide circles, calling to each other in their high echoing voices. By March, the fledgling comes to perch on my children's old swing set, practicing flight lessons from one low perch to the ground and back. Nearby, the Spanish bluebells I planted on the graves of my old pets are blooming.

I love this house and these woods. And this year, the man I was married to for almost thirty years, the father of my children—the man who built that swing set and once helped bury one of those old dogs—is taking me to court to try to take this home where we raised our children, where our daughters still spend vacations—away.

Watching, more often hearing, that family of hawks, even after five years of divorce, it is baffling to me to see how this has happened to my own family. Reminding me of my own daughters when they would put on their own plays for their father and me, the fledgling has gotten the hang of flying and flies and calls constantly. Though I gained a degree in zoology in the days when we tried not to anthropomorphize animals, I have given that up over the years of observing as a mother and a writer, so I am sure the fledgling is calling, "Look at me, Mom. Look at me!"

I tell my grown girls about watching the fledgling hawk. Elaine, my oldest, says she likes to know where I am so she can picture me there. I think of that now as I try to write something. I would like to picture myself somewhere too. It used to be so easy to picture myself—at the typewriter and then the computer, in the kitchen cooking dinner, on the back porch, cheering on the children. Later, I was always in the car, or at a music concert or lessons for Elaine, a pianist; or taking my youngest, Lynn, to her myriad of high school activities. "If there is a sign-up list," her dad and I joked, "Lynn's name is on it."

But now, none of this seems to matter to Joseph, who has shouted to me about so many things, "I don't remember that at all." His eyes glaze over as a dog's might when it is threatened and going to bite.

I tell my lawyer later that I would much rather have been in a room with a pack of wild wolves, because wolves I understand. I think I could soothe a wolf and not get bitten. But I cannot soothe the man that one of our counselors called "the love of your life."

That man is dead, swallowed whole, by the monster of addiction.

Spring, 2010
Survival Snapshot: Evil Eye

The first time I heard the term, sexual addiction, I laughed. A college friend had come to visit my husband and me, bringing along her six-year-old daughter. Our girls were five and seven, so all of the girls were outside playing. Then, we lived in another house in another state, also with woods behind it. I had hoped to live in that home the moment I heard a Kentucky warbler singing in the woods. At that time I was writing a book about animal neighbors, and the song seemed a sign. I still believe in signs, but perhaps more now as a source of pointing us in some direction of survival and growth rather than in storybook happy endings.

Our friend, Joy, told us how her sister was recovering from sex addiction—and that is when I laughed, with an innocence I look back on as both a blessed time and one when I wonder if I missed ominous signs. "You can't be addicted to sex," I said, echoed by my husband. I think now that he knew he had problems then even if I had missed them, but I don't think he really recognized the addictive aspects of that monster growing within him.

Joy widened her eyes and said, "Oh, yes, you can." Now, I recognize that tone of frustration and horror that "no one gets this" in her voice, but then, I thought she was being dramatic. This was the same friend who had told me when she divorced a few years earlier that her husband was emotionally abusive.

I had had the good sense then not to laugh, but I didn't understand emotional abuse either. Certainly, I didn't understand that those seeds were sprouting in my own marriage even then, but had not grown fully enough for me to guess they were taking over the garden.

Joy went on to tell us how her sister had gone from partner to partner—one night stand to one night stand—until finally finding the recovery to marry and have a child. Now, I wonder if her sister stayed in recovery. I hope so. Recovery followed by relapse is one of the cruelest parts of being in love with an addicted person.

Though now I wonder if there ever was complete recovery for my husband, there were at least three times when I thought—and I think he at least *wanted* to do right as a husband and father—recovery had been made. It was that hope that kept us together. Still, I am wondering if that was the best that could be managed. It has seemed to me that even God cannot change certain things without our cooperation, once they are set in motion. If we continually harden our hearts, perhaps they become impenetrable even to God. However, I have come to believe that God can adjust the timing in answer to our prayers.

Elaine said, when I told her of the latest court battle with her father to change our divorce agreement for the third time, "Thank God this didn't happen when we were little. Think of the custody battles." I said, "If he had been this way when you were little, the three of us would have been fleeing place to place through Canada. I would never have left you alone with him as he is now."

For a minute, we debated on whether this would have been smart or not, but then we laughed because that time has safely passed. I can lose my home, and my mother and my friends will worry about my life, but my children are safely grown. They are though my children, and that mother instinct is still present. I think of elephants and their matriarchal herds, of how mothers and daughters stay together and if separated, recognize each other again after long periods.

Three people now, besides myself, have seen that glazed look in Joseph's eyes that lets you know my former husband could snap. My children have not seen it and I am grateful for this, yet afraid—afraid the monster will erupt on them unawares. I tell Elaine when her father visits not to mention me, though I cannot see how he can look at either of our girls and not see me in them. Maybe though he sees me at an earlier time before he felt all of that guilt and anger towards me. I have realized that he will never forgive me for how badly he messed up!

Once, in an exercise at our church, we were asked to write down people we knew that we thought had the qualities of living saints. One of the girls came running to tell me that "Daddy put down your name as a saint." I don't remember being so much flattered as startled. I am certainly not a saint. I can blow up with the best of them. As my mother always says, "She doesn't have that red hair for nothing." Certainly my husband, of all people, knew this. I am kind and compassionate, which are good qualities, but I think this translated at some level to my husband as that no matter what he did I would love him and stay with him. And on some level, he was right. I still love the man inside that monster, but I wouldn't stay with the monster and become the next meal, or a monster myself.

And so when I tried to explain in a mediation meeting that even if I sold the house (one thing he wanted, so he could have more money from it), I thought there wouldn't be much equity in the present down market and because the house needed repairs I couldn't afford, he shouted at me, "I wouldn't know what the house is like because you won't let me come over anymore!" Why would he want to visit?

Maybe he sometimes does remember us in our marriage before the addiction monster had grown to take over the man—when all I saw was a toddler monster having an occasional temper tantrum that I then attributed to low blood sugar or stress. I was too busy taking care of real children then. I wonder now if I was just too tired and busy, or if it was love-blindness for my entire little family.

My eighty-three-year-old mother went along with me and my friend, Ruth, to the mediation, and sat in the waiting room. Mother, who had not seen Joseph since before our separation seven years ago, was determined to "look at him." She wanted him to have to face someone in my family. I wore a Greek amulet against the evil eye to the mediation so we could laugh about Mother's evil eye not splashing over on me.

During the mediation, when I asked to speak to the mediator alone and it was Joseph's turn to wait, he said, "I'm not going out there with your mother and your friend!" I saw the mediator trying to suppress a smile as he suggested there was a kitchen in the other direction where Joseph could wait. After the mediation—three hours of Joseph insisting he got a bad deal, that he "can't remember that at all" the agreements and promises he made, that there was no need to go into "that" (*that* being repeated infidelities)—we finally called it quits, having gotten nowhere. Then he refused to leave the room. Mom walked into the room and stared at him. I thought this was funny—even the mediator grinned—until Mom told me the next morning, "Now, I see what you have been talking about. He is so consumed with rage and hatred—he would kill you if he could."

Spring, 2010
Survival Snapshot: Gun, Convent, Broken Heart

I know that I shouldn't tell Clay, the man in my life now, about what Mom said about Joseph looking as though he could kill me. I know this will again bring up the conversation about why won't I buy a gun and let him teach me how to shoot. Why won't I defend myself? He, a former law officer and a man that grew up on a farm where if a predator was going to attack you or your family, you shot it, will insist that I need to be tougher. I have explained to him that I cannot shoot the father of my children, no matter what.

But I do tell him, and he does bring up the gun argument. And I conclude that the man I was married to for almost thirty years thinks I am a witch, and the man that has been a true friend—a gift—to me during these recent years thinks I am a wimp.

I wonder again if my original thought on divorce—joining a convent—is the decision I should have made. As an Episcopalian, I would possibly have had that option. In fact it is not the first time I have thought of it. Before I married, I wondered if this might be my calling. I love gardens, like to study, do a lot of praying—and I have been told too many times that I am "too good a person." (I wonder now if that is just a code expression for wimp.)

But love—love for a man, love for being in the middle of this community, love for all of my old books, and perhaps most of all love for having a dog for company—has always kept me from choosing that cloister calling. Perhaps before I married Joseph, it was mostly love for that man and love for having children that kept me from the convent. But after the divorce, I read in the newsletter that I get from an Episcopal sisterhood that divorced or widowed women can still join. My friends thought I was kidding when I discussed this option, and my daughters weren't keen at all on the idea of "my mother, the nun." But it was the thought of my old dachshund, Wilbur, and my old misnamed tuxedo tomcat, Charlotte, being abandoned that honestly kept me from fully considering the convent at this time. The cat might have adapted to convent gardens, but Wilbur and I were a pair, and I doubted I could get the dispensation for a dachshund to sleep with me. After each of the girls had left home for college and then "Daddy" left, or was forced to leave home (depending on the lens seen through), the dog and cat had stuck to me. I called them Glue and Super Glue.

The cat did cat-like anxiety things like scratch the wallpaper and urinate on the carpet, while the dog refused to eat until I picked him up and fed him by hand. Wilbur developed a tumor that I had removed and typical old dog teeth that had to be pulled. (You know you are on your own when you find yourself meeting the vet at midnight with a sick dog after driving a long country road with no one knowing you have left home.) And so we had survived too much together—Wilbur, Charlotte, and me—for me to join a convent and not have them with me.

But now, my old animals have died within the last year. Wilbur, the dachshund, died first at fifteen and then Charlotte, the cat, three months later. The cat supposedly died of a long-dormant cat virus and kidney failure. I though will always believe my cat, Charlotte, died of a broken heart.

Spring, 2010
Survival Snapshot: Highway

"A broken heart doesn't kill you, even when you wish it would," I repeated to myself day after day after I learned that Joseph had betrayed me with multiple visits to massage parlors and "gentleman's clubs." I had not known this until the twenty-sixth year of our marriage. Only after fifteen years of marriage did I learn about the hidden pornography, and the adult bookstores—that discovery finally made by a second set of 900 number phone calls.

Just as I laughed the first time my friend told me there was such a thing as sexual addiction, I have found it next to impossible to explain to those who have not experienced it what sex addiction does to a marriage, to the addict's spouse, to a family. Partners of alcoholics and drug addicts understand the best. I have lost count of the number of people who have asked me if my ex-husband is on drugs. I have that explanation I have learned down pretty well, though I know I sigh when I start it: that the biochemicals in our own brains can become as potent of drugs as any others, that in someone vulnerable to this addiction that those early exposures are like wandering down a narrow road, perhaps even one taken by mistake, but that with each hit of guilty excitement, the path in his or her own brain gets wider and wider until he is on the LA freeway with no way to get off unless willing to make a tremendous effort.

What I learned as a partner of someone that kept detouring onto that freeway is that ultimately it doesn't matter who he runs down, or even who is in the car with him as he careens down that road. But the strangest thing about it is how long the family can be kept in the dark about this obsession—how long he can keep the racecar hidden in an invisible garage until it takes on a mind of its own and bursts through the house, wrecking everyone in its way.

Sexual addiction has nothing to do with not having enough sex with your intimate partner—in fact, it has more to do with avoiding real connection with someone you love in order to have a false momentary thrill with someone in a picture or a voice on a phone, to eventually paying someone the addict will never see again or showing up at the door of someone he met on the internet. One counselor explained to me that the addict is so afraid of real connection that this is ironically thought of as safe sex.

I have learned to understand this in my mind, but my heart still doesn't get it. To me, it seemed like guzzling rubbing alcohol rather than having a fine wine. It felt like my husband had urinated into the communion wine.

Beyond the physical betrayal, the subsequent fear of disease, the money I eventually realized had been drained away piece by piece from the accounts, there is the lying. This is the worst. This is what made me begin to doubt my own sanity, to doubt my own life, to wonder—and keep wondering—what was real about this person I had married, lived with, raised children with—loved.

Years ago, when the first group of 900 number sex calls showed up on a phone bill, I honestly thought it was some kind of crazy computer mix-up. The children and I had been at the zoo on the Saturday when the calls were posted, and my husband was supposed to have been at work. I called the phone company and took on the poor representative, insisting no one had been home but the dog. She reluctantly took off the bills, but clearly didn't believe me. We had recently moved to a different house and I began to wonder if someone had a key, maybe workmen; or I finally even considered one of my close friend's fifteen-year-old son who took care of our dog and had a key. And I was worried about the boy. He was going through that fifteen-year-old time of rebellion (what I later called "the armpit of parenting" when my own daughters went through it). He had been one of my favorite writing students; his mom was my friend, and I wondered if I should mention this possibility to her.

This was my first direct evidence of the monster now being in control of the racecar, though I was still wearing a blindfold in the car. In fact, I didn't even realize the family station wagon had turned into this crazy racecar. Maybe love does make us blind, or maybe I was just married to a good liar. The best liars are those who have lied to themselves so long that they really don't know the truth. (Years later, when one counselor tried lie-detector tests with my husband to keep him off the sex addiction highway, he beat at least some of the tests themselves.)

I certainly didn't want to accuse my student or worry his mother if the phone calls had nothing to do with him, so I asked Joseph a second time if he had made the calls. Having no idea what I was dealing with, I wasn't even upset if he had. No woman has been married for fifteen years without figuring out men are different than women and certainly can have different feelings about sex. "Just tell me if you made them," I said, "anyone can be curious about what these are like." At that point, I had enough faith in him, enough faith in my marriage, that I didn't even feel threatened if he had made the calls.

Joseph categorically denied he had made the calls. "Do you think I should talk to Susan?" I asked. "I don't want Brian to get hooked on this stuff."

"Go ahead if you want to," he said.

I am thankful that I decided not to talk to my friend Susan about this, but to this day I am astounded that a man in his forties, a father of two children, would allow a fifteen-year-old boy to be confronted with making sex calls rather then to admit that he made them himself.

What I didn't realize then was that in at least this arena of responsibility, my husband had developed or kept the mindset of a fifteen-year-old boy himself—perhaps of even a child—rather than that of a mature man.

Every counselor we saw, starting with Ben, after a second set of 900 sex call numbers appeared on the family phone, and ending a decade later with Penny, when I knew Joseph's sex addiction ultimately included massage parlors and one-night stands with strangers, said to me within a session, "This has nothing to do with you—it's all about his mother."

Did I find this reassuring in the beginning? I think I did when, whether it was about his mother or not, I still thought my love—our love— would be enough to overcome whatever had happened or not happened in my husband's childhood. We all need that parenting that gives us all an inner assurance of love—we are crippled without that assurance. But by the end of our marriage, when Joseph seemed to mistake me for his mother, accusing me of saying things—or at least thinking things—she might have said, I began to feel stranded on that highway between the man and his mother and he kept running me over, trying to get to her.

During this long ending of our marriage, I went with my younger daughter, Lynn, as a chaperone on what I think of as the youth group trip from hell—and a trip that I imagine set back interdenominational youth work between the Baptist churches in Florida and the Episcopal church a good fifty years.

The kids, another mom, and our leaders were supposed to stay in an old—and I do mean old—Baptist church camp. The idea was that the kids would help with camp repairs and of course have the requisite time to visit the beach and Walt Disney World. Along with my daughter and one other girl, the rest of the trip included five teenage boys. The Baptist youth groups included a number a teenage girls, including the lovely daughter of one youth leader. Their leader, if not a retired Marine sergeant, certainly gave a good impression of one. Our boys were of course immediately admiring the young ladies. And this of course was a recipe for disaster!

The day that our kids and other leaders were going to the beach, I took a little research trip to the Seminole Indian country. I came back by evening, hot and tired and informed, to sense some kind of tension in the camp—but, being accustomed to tension, I didn't pay much attention. The other mom and I got our two charges into bed (or more accurately, they got us old moms into bed) in the little cabin reserved for the female division of our youth group.

In spite of the heat and the bugs, and an occasional question about the possibility of mice, I was tired enough to sleep on my pre-World War II bunk until two in the early morning, when there was a definite pounding on the cabin door. I woke up expecting fire or alligators, but looked out to see a circle in front of our cabin with the youth leader of the lovely daughter, alternately intoning forgiveness and condemnation for our boys for thoughts of fornication—or worse.

When I reached to turn on the light, the other mom stopped me with, "No! They'll know we're in here." And just at this particular moment, I felt a furious biting on my legs, which I later learned were fire ants. But as I stated earlier, I always have had a little more confidence in dealing with angry animals that humans, so I brushed at my legs and the four of us huddled around the window, trying to figure out what was going on. I had this bizarre flash of what Hester Pryne in The Scarlet Letter must have felt among her Puritan neighbors.

The cell phone rang with our youth leader whispering that he was taking the boys out of the camp—upon the angry, Marine-like youth leader's demand—right that moment, but we girls could stay until the morning. The story was that while our kids were at the beach, some of the local kids had been working on their cabin and had found a Playboy magazine and a condom, that I imagine was largely for show for the other boys, among one of our kid's stuff. Then, after supper, our boys somehow got the bright idea of dragging an old couch from the cabin down to the dock. Our youth group leader, naturally exhausted from a day with teens and used to the antics of boys, was nodding off and not paying attention. (If you've chaperoned many youth groups, you know that at some points your main concern is that the kids not end up in a bar, get eaten by alligators, or kidnapped by aliens—anything else, you figure you can handle when you are awake again.) Then, the boys got the further bright idea of peeking in the cabin windows of one of the girls' cabins—naturally the cabin with the lovely daughter of the burley youth leader.

The girls began screaming and ran to Dad/leader and thus, by two in the morning, the story had become that our Playboy-loving, condom-toting boys had pulled the couch down to the dock in order to drag the girls onto said couch and have their way with them.

The girls were in hysterics, fueled by an angry father who had by then convinced them their virtue had barely been saved; our boys and fearless leader had fled (with the church credit card) on the way to the local hotel, and the four females from our group were standing looking at a group of people holding candles and pounding on our cabin door. It was so hot in that cabin that I thought I might faint, but we were afraid to open the door!

When the prayer circle dispersed, I announced to my co-mom that we were getting out of here—not staying the night. "These people," I said, "could go crazy." So we all, thankfully having a car still remaining, spent the night shopping in the twenty-four-hour Walmart. In the morning, we trudged to the home of our hosts, a wonderful Baptist minister and his wife—an older couple with a sense of humor—ate breakfast, and somehow made it to Walt Disney World.

Although I have pictures of my daughter with Mickey Mouse, I don't remember much of that day. I do remember the cast-down looks of our teenage boys, especially one that I doubt had ever gotten in trouble before in his life (obviously not the one with the Playboy). I remember hoping that this was a chance to give the kids some perspective—to do what I wished had been done for my husband as a teen, who had learned to hide anything to do with sex rather than just accept it as a part of life—something we can use at least some sense about, rather than guzzling it like cheap rubbing alcohol in an alley. I told the boys that this had been silly, but it wasn't necessary to rehearse it over and over in their minds (for glory or shame), that they should just learn something from it about thinking before you drag a couch to the dock and sneak up to a window in the dark—and then let it go.

We somehow made it back home from that trip, and a few days later I was telling my husband what I now thought of as one of those funny life stories. When I got to the part about trying to give the boys some perspective, he blurted out, "So, you told them they should be totally ashamed of how they'd acted—that they were scum."

I was taken aback. "No," I said, "why would I have said that? Have I ever been that way with our kids or anyone else's kids?"

His eyes had that glazed look and he was looking past me to something, or someone, I couldn't see. "It's what you were thinking," he said.

And I realized, in a moment more frightening than peering out the window of that cabin at a mob, that he wasn't hearing or seeing me, but his own mother. I realized that emotionally the man had become a cringing—and very angry—kid, and that he truly didn't see me anymore, but an angry mother. And he was determined to get back at that mother.

Spring, 2010
Survival Snapshot: Recognizing the Vampire

Each counselor, each book I was asked to read, each program I watched on sex addiction, said that a high percentage—over ninety percent—of people with this addiction were abused in some way as a child—largely sexual abuse—though possibly emotional, physical, or the abuse of neglect.

As with everything else, I can only write from my perspective—what I saw and heard—perhaps most of all what I felt. This is especially true of my husband's childhood. I wasn't there! However, I do believe that the effects of that childhood were the basis for the cracks in the foundation of his ability of connect with our family. Those cracks shrank and widened in the land of our marriage, sometimes such narrow cracks that certainly I and perhaps Joseph didn't even know they existed. They widened at times, and the land shook and then settled down again. But eventually, for reasons I don't fully understand and never will (though I have some good guesses), the original fault line finally broke apart the land we had built together, leaving a landscape strangely dominated by the sex addiction super highway.

My former mother-in-law is a vampire. This is a harsh metaphor and I feel cruel using it. I am a mother myself, and for most of my adult life I hoped to have a good relationship with my husband's mother. Actually, I think we had the best of what relationship was possible for many of those years. At times I barely felt the blood of my emotions being drained away. What I especially didn't see was her son, bite by bite, becoming a vampire himself.

Perhaps it would be kinder to compare her to a vampire bat—a creature that is born that way and through no fault of its own, must drink the blood of others for nourishment. But this comparison does not hold. The genetic basis of our personalities grows ever more fascinating with new scientific discoveries, strengthening the old debate of nature versus nurture. I don't think you can dismiss either—I have seen too much the evidence of both.

I know a little of my mother-in-law's childhood—a childhood in the Great Depression, a father who gambled away household money, a mother who was trying to cope with a large Catholic family. Once she told me how her mother used to hide when the man who collected the small amount due on a life insurance policy would come to the door monthly. Her own mother died when my mother-in-law was young, and she and her sisters raised a younger brother.

I know that when my husband was a young teenager, his mother's father lived with them for certain periods, and that she put her son in the basement to sleep and gave her father his room. When we were married, Joseph used to cover up his face to sleep, telling me he had grown used to sleeping that way because the basement was cold. I don't think this was abuse, or even neglect, but what I think is that any discomfort was simply not acknowledged. And maybe I, being the mother of daughters, am seeing this entirely differently than it was. There seemed, though, to me, a pattern of alternating adoration of the only son and total neglect of family support that existed as long as I was in this family.

Once when we were visiting, a discussion came up about a priest accused of child molestation. "I thought," my mother-in-law said, "he was an absolute saint." We talked about how people had different faces and it wasn't easy to tell. Then she said, "Well, even if it's true, I don't see why the church should have to pay all of this money. After all, he didn't really hurt those little boys—he just touched them."

Years later we received an email from a former classmate from the Catholic boys school where my husband had attended, asking for letters of support for a teacher—a priest—accused of molesting students. The man was a teacher when my husband attended the school as a boy. Whether the man was guilty or not, I don't know. But in the midst of knowing this as a root cause of sexual addiction, of course I still wonder if such could have happened to my husband when young. We were encouraged in counseling to explore these possibilities.

If this had been discovered about one of my own children's teachers after their school years, I would have talked to them to be sure it had not affected them. I would have acknowledged something that could have had a lasting affect, so I thought that surely my mother-in-law knew nothing about these accusations. The next time we talked, I asked her if she remembered this teacher. She told me the accusations had been in the paper for months.

She had never thought if this could have hurt her son, yet this is the woman who kept exact count of every time we were late to a family gathering, who announced she would only visit for the same amount of time that we had visited her, and was furious the year we arrived on Christmas Day rather than Christmas Eve because we had spent the previous day with one of my best friends and her husband because the husband was dying with lung cancer and would not see another Christmas.

The holidays—not just Christmas, but some exact time (that was never given, but which I figured out over the years was usually, though not always, four in the afternoon on everything from Christmas Eve to Groundhog's Day)—were command appearances with my mother-in-law, no matter what else was happening in our lives.

Such demands I think must stem from insecurity about if anyone loves you—if they are there on command, that seems some kind of proof of love. Or back to the vampire image, if a victim exposes his vulnerability—his neck in vampire terms, and lets the insecure vampire take a bite, she owns not just his love but his soul. And such emotional vampires are perhaps born with that tendency, or perhaps made that way by their own lives. I am only a writer, a zoologist, a mother myself—and so I make no claims to anything beyond what I think, from what happened in my own life.

I knew that these demands—this never getting it quite right, was draining the joy in much of my life. But it took me a long time to realize I never would get it right because there was no real right to get.

When my youngest sister-in-law got married the first time, it was the classic big wedding and we were told in no uncertain terms that no children were welcome to ruin the big day. Though a nursery could have been set up, this just didn't seem to occur to any of the family but me, and I had learned by then to not make my silly suggestions.

Elaine was a baby at the time, and we dutifully got a babysitter for the wedding and reception. We went to the wedding, the reception, and then arrived as commanded at a little family supper back at the house—at which point my sister-in-law burst into tears and my mother-in-law moaned, "You didn't bring the baby. We wanted her here." And though I see now that Joseph or I should have said, "Tough," my husband and I went back to our house, almost an hour away, picked up our daughter, and returned with her to the family supper.

What I also remember about this wedding is that while pictures were being taken of the family, my mother-in-law told me to move out of the way so she could get pictures of her children together. My father had recently died, and I felt suddenly very alone, but I stood out of the way of the camera. If she had then included me in another picture, that would have made such a difference, but she didn't. When the wedding pictures came back my mother-in-law commented that it was so strange that I was in none of the pictures.

Summer , 2010
Survival Snapshot: Reframing—Reclaiming

Reframing family photos to focus on my daughters, our pets, and those people who continued to be part of my life now, was the first reclaiming I learned to do. It was the first place after my husband and I separated that I could begin to reshape my own life, trying somehow to honor the life we had created together—especially our beautiful daughters—and yet move forward from that point into my own life as a single mother and a free woman.

This is not an easy task. I think of those fairy tale heroines having to pick up every grain of rice or spin a room of straw into gold. Always in those stories, there is help—birds that pluck up the rice, a dwarf that spins straw into gold (and then tries to take the firstborn child)! Some help is more generous than others! Still, you take what you can get at the time.

Anger has often been my dwarf during this process—what has finally allowed me to tear up the legion of apology cards from my husband from the last days of our marriage. Those straw apologies were never destined to turn into gold for there was no real substance in them. Sad creatures that I cannot even think of a metaphor to describe, and the angel of survival, are what have helped me pack away the earlier years of photographs and cards that I believe did mean something, and of inscribed books and jewelry, into the cave-like closet under my stairs, thinking time might transform these back into treasures for our children or grandchildren.

And, yes, I have had more birds, more angels, more godmothers, during this time than dwarves. I think of all of this today because of a weekend, five years now after my divorce and another couple of years, more or less after the big bang of my husband finally confessing that he had actually paid women and "let them touch" him and that now he wanted to "see who was out there." Such a conversation is a rough memory snapshot, but today I am writing about the photos that matter now—the ones that made it back into frames, the ones I am still making—many on what my children call "the wall of daughters."

My dear friend Ruth and I had dinner Saturday night. Having had her own marriage and divorce trials, she has sometimes understood more than my other dear friends, still married or widowed—though I would not take gold for any single one! I asked her to read the first pages of this recollection.

A recollection is what I am calling this book, so different than any other writing I have done. It is not an autobiography because I am at least hoping to have a lot more of life to live. Though I suppose it will be shelved in the memoir section, memoir sounds too official to me. These are recollections, filtered through my own memory and life, as true as I can remember. Yet memory and changing perspectives aren't fact checkers— they are what stand out to me for how I got here and how I keep going— what I frame and what I pack away to see what happens through more time—what history makes of these artifacts. Ruth called them snapshots, and that I think is another term I can use. The angle of the photographer makes all of the difference in the pictures we take. We avoid the gas station next to the white country church in the photo, and when we look back at that photo, sometimes we don't even remember the gas station was there. And sometimes we do—and think now that the contrast would've made the picture better.

Another dear friend, Dora, shared my child-raising years, she and I spending weekend evenings talking after children were tucked into bed after a day of adventure. She has been my confidant for over thirty years. After Ruth's comments on Saturday, Dora said the next day, "You've developed a lot of survival skills over these years. Someone ought to benefit from them."

I hope that is true, yet I am not writing a self-help book with steps to take. I have read and found helpful many of these books, yet I have found that while some rough maps through this terrain at least give you a place to start, there are lots of holes and detours only in your journey that only you can negotiate—and it is on-the-job training. Still, I hope there is value in simply showing the journey—and the survival. This photo album of snapshots is one thing I have to give my daughters and my readers.

Summer, 2010
Survival Snapshot: Mining Dreams and Dinners

Once you've been in a car crash, it is easier to recognize for others the danger signals you missed yourself. When I see younger women, passengers in the car, struggling to accept the early signs of a husband moving onto the sex addiction highway, I want to scream, "Jump out now, honey!"

But I don't. I don't respond to letters in advice columns or blogs for television shows where a young woman with a baby is already weeping because her husband surfs for porn while watching the baby, though I do sigh and yell at the television set a lot—every day.

Every day, it seems there is another announcement of a celebrity or political figure in the midst of a sex scandal. Every day, there is a television show somewhere that shows a young weeping woman, or a middle-aged woman in shock. It is easy for me to yell at the older woman to jump out—I could give classes in surviving the jump.

But I don't know what to advise a young woman. It does seem that a great many infidelities begin with the easy access to pornography followed quickly by the next addiction step, into chat rooms and sites with names like "Infidelities Are Us. C'mon in!"

My husband, in the pre-internet days, took, I think, a slow ride into full-blown addiction. I have often wondered if this easy internet infidelity access hadn't come along, if he could have at least managed not to crash the car. I don't know this, but it worries me to see the easy gateway to infidelity available now for so many young couples, and to see this almost-acceptance of getting away with it. Women, younger and older, are now more aware of the problem, but I am not sure any wiser about how to deal with it.

And that would be the point—I learned the spouse can't deal with this addiction beyond surviving for herself and her children, within or outside of the marriage. She (or he, for this can go the other way) can try to support the person she loves in recovery. But she can't do the recovery for him. Whether to tell her to jump out at the first sign, or keep trying to navigate with a map that keeps folding up on her, I don't know.

I know that this addiction can begin long before a marriage starts and will continue after the marriage (or marriages) ends. Near the end of our marriage, my husband told me one morning at breakfast that he had had a dream he remembered.

I dream in novels and series, as do my daughters. When they are home, we can sit at the breakfast table for an hour, comparing last night's dreams. But Joseph hardly ever remembered a dream.

"I was standing," he began, "at the entrance to what looked like a mine shaft, staring down into that darkness, afraid to go down. You came towards me holding a hard hat. 'Go down and it will be alright,' you said. But I just couldn't do it."

I said, "I think if you could go down there and see what is below the ground, you could get better." He just shrugged.

I think now that this was the point where he quit trying—the point where the addiction monster began to grow so large that it could swallow the man. For years, the monster had taken nibbles and bites, but the man was still there—wounded, bandaged, but still the man I knew. When he gave up that quest of going down into the mine with that safety hat of counseling and friendship, and yes, my love, the monster began to swallow whole limbs.

But, then, I was still trying to hand him protective gear—and if I could have, I believe I would have gone below ground with him to help him find a way through that darkness. But this was not my journey to take. This is perhaps the hardest thing to realize when you love someone. This mine was dug long before you came along, and while you can help the person you love with hard hats and oxygen and encouragement and a hand to help them back up once they've tunneled through the mine, you just aren't the miner for this mine.

I remember once when I took our teenage daughter to counseling, my mother-in-law laughed at me. "I never wanted to bother with that stuff for my kids," she said. "I didn't want to spend all of that money." I have thought many times that the entire family has certainly paid far more than for any investment she might have made in my husband's childhood. I do not know if counseling as a teen would have helped my husband, though I do think counseling would have given him a fighting chance against that developing monster. I felt with my own kids that if I could at least point them early in the direction of help—from professional counseling to being able to talk to me or a friend to certainly spiritual guidance and prayer, I could at least send them off with a survival kit. For we all have mines to explore, some deeper than others, some with a lot of rubble and some with perhaps hidden rubies or buried treasure. If we can't go down, we can't really find out what is in us, what has made us for good and bad, what we are. We can't find the treasure, or even the coal to keep us warm, unless we get through the soot and grit.

Around the time of that dream, my husband became obsessed with the idea that I wasn't giving him unconditional love. Somewhere down the road, I finally realized that this meant, "I do whatever I want to do, and you just live with it even if what I do puts you at mental, spiritual, and physical risk." Even now, I think we are in that same place—well, he is in that same place toward me, furious that I am not making his life run smoothly. "He seems," my lawyer says, "to think it was your responsibility to negotiate a bad deal for yourself." And I am sure that is just what he thinks. Across that mediation table, I can feel the manipulation as he repeats that he got a bad deal, that he has been treated unfairly. He looks at me, expecting me as I did I see now too often in our marriage, to take over and fix the accounts or deal with the kids, or deal with anyone outside of his day-to-day work, especially his own family.

On Joseph's forty-second birthday, I had the bright idea of having a nice extended family dinner. I planned the menu for the food he wanted, baked the cake, bought the big candles with a four and a two. And then my mother-in-law quit speaking to my youngest sister-in-law, who was now getting married for the second time. This was not the first time my mother-in-law had quit speaking to her children. The reason this time for her to quit speaking was that the groom was divorced and not a Catholic. There was always a reason where she didn't have to admit, "You're leaving me—and I don't like it!"

Now I should have just called off the dinner and had a special meal with our little family. But while four counselors and as many ministers have assured me that I am not the dreaded "co-dependent," I do think I got an extra dose of the nurturing gene. Contrary to the theory that we are attracted to someone like a parent, one counselor explained that sometimes we are attracted to someone who has what a parent was missing. She said my nurturing qualities were something Joseph had craved from his own mother. What is hard is the balance. Nurturing, forgiveness, compassion—these are good qualities. But when the spouse or even the entire family takes advantage of these good qualities, then you—good qualities and all, are bound and gagged with the ropes you thought you were just extending to pull someone to safety.

So, no, I didn't call off the dinner. Thinking the extended family would pull together for Joseph's birthday, I went ahead with plans. My sister-in-law showed up at two in the afternoon. I can't remember what, but I offered her something to eat and drink and settled down to visit until my mother and father-in-law arrived. But she left before they came, and so we had the birthday dinner in shifts. It was a defeating day.

I think the saddest part, for me, of Joseph's addiction is that I had seen therapy begin to work for my husband; but when he lapsed back, the monster was in full control. After the long-ago discovery of the second set of evidence of 900 calls, and the subsequent revelations that there was a secret stash of pornography magazines and videos in the basement, we went to our first counselor.

Ben was a younger man with nervous twitches that would grow worse as the hour progressed. He was easy to talk to, and was single himself. I have been consistently surprised how many marriage counselors are single themselves, but I also know it is sometimes easier to see how to win a battle when you are not in the middle of one yourself! He immediately diagnosed sexual addiction and we sat there, stunned.

Ben advised us to get as far away from Joseph's mother as possible (yes, Joseph did have a father, and I'll get to him in another snapshot). At this time, we were arranging a job change, begun before all hell broke loose in our marriage. We were moving a state away, but Ben advised us to move across the country to Montana!

I don't think either of us quite believed in actual sexual addiction with this first counselor, but I at least began to see the possibility. I wasn't laughing anymore.

There is still a debate among professionals about whether this is a true disease, and I think the prevalence of calling everything from texting to shopping an addiction makes us take real addictions less seriously. A nun in a conference I attended even wondered if she were addicted to crossword puzzles.

As the years passed, Joseph would turn around and accuse me of being addicted to everything from buying ink pens (I am talking Bic pens here—the kind every mom keeps—packages of five pens for a dollar when her kids are in school) to books. Now, I do love books. I work with the library sale where I live, and all of the folks of my Friends of the Library organization laugh about our overflowing shelves and piles of books on our floors, and watch our customers run in with suitcases to fill with books when the sale opens on Friday morning. We all have friends who can't pass the shoe table or new dishes or jewelry counter without looking. The man now in my life does flint knapping, more commonly known as making arrowheads, and we laugh that he is addicted to rocks. We also agree that I can live with him piling up rocks to knap and he can live with me bringing home books for reading and research. Of course, it helps that we live in two separate houses!

The point, though, is to figure out what makes your life, both within yourself and with those you love, richer—and what strips life away. When my girls were teenagers, first vulnerable to drugs and alcohol and questioning how to know what was just a good time and what could get them into a lifetime of trouble, I came up with a definition that has at least worked for me beyond all of the scientific definitions of what is a real addiction. I explained that if something took you out of yourself to where you felt you were having an extraordinary experience and when you returned to the ordinary day, you were better for this—more thoughtful, kinder, could see an original way to solve a problem, you were most likely dealing with not an addiction, but a passion that was worth pursuing. Such things as poetry, prayer, books, even certain movies and games fall in this category. Shopping for shoes, unless you are truly breaking the bank, seems to me pretty neutral. Also, if the passion affects your relationships for the better, you are probably in good shape. Recently, Clay and I went to the midwest's largest charity book sale, where we found several treasures, and then went to a little shop that specialized in flavors of balsamic vinegar and olive oil. Clay loves balsamic vinegar and tasted the varieties like at a wine tasting. He finally settled on the Tuscan olive oil and the eighteen-year-old balsamic vinegar. "When my tomatoes come in," he said, "I'll make you a salad." Open things like this that you share with your partner, your friends, your better self seem to me healthy passions. Sure, he already has bottles of vinegar and heaven knows I have plenty of books, but no one needed to hide anything, break the bank, etc. And when I read the books and share some thoughts, when he shares his tomato salad with me, we will have shared this experience even more.

The inability to share something with those you love is one clue to what is an addiction. Addictions tend to first be hidden from those that are really important in our lives, or indulged in with other addicts, each spinning in his own realm. And when we come back to ordinary life—if we can come back to ordinary life—we are usually sick and ashamed, and hiding this from those we love. It is the difference between someone who enjoys a glass of wine with a gourmet dinner with friends and someone who drinks anything for a high to where he could be drinking cough syrup instead of the fine wine, and then gets in the car and drives. Eventually, I think, even the shame blurs and he will drive that car with his friends, even his children inside, shouting the whole time that it is his life and he will do what he wants.

This is, I know, a simple definition beyond all of the biology and cultural possibilities of what is acceptable, but it is the one I come back to: if you and those you love are better for the passion, go for it; if you are sick and hurting others, ashamed and hiding one minute and blustering that no one owns you the next, think again.

Yet when is the point when the person no longer thinks and the addiction is totally in control? This must vary with different people, and then we are back to brain chemistry and genetics, but I have seen addiction become in control.

With that first counselor, who had total confidence we could get through this together, I thought everything would be okay. One puzzle piece, though, that Joseph never admitted to me or any counselor until the last of our marriage, was that he wasn't just looking at many forms of pornography, he was visiting what I jokingly (the kind of joke which you use so you laugh instead of cry) call "women of the flesh."

I know now that the first time my husband visited a woman he paid for sexual contact—well, the first time that he has told me about—was before I even discovered the 900 phone calls on our bill. My husband bullied me every year into going on his own on a vacation to a tournament to play war games—not the kind you dress up for, but the ones on boards, where this time through strategy, the South might win the Civil War. Hindsight really is twenty/twenty. When I would say anything about the kids and me never having a vacation, he would lament how he never had any nights out with the boys, this was his one hobby. (One time, the girls and I did go on the trip. Joseph shouted at us to get up at six in the morning, wanted little to do with us, and was extremely irritable. He made it a trip I at least never wanted to take again.) He would begin this campaign several months ahead and finally wear me down, until I actually believed this was fair and was defending him to his own mother.

I know now that real nights out with the boys would have been a much better outlet, because I have learned that men with sexual addictions rarely have good male friends. But, again, hindsight is perfect. What I didn't know was that these trips included forays into local adult bookstores and movies and eventually visiting those women of the flesh.

I remember well what happened to our family at home during the first trip where Joseph much later told me he had paid for sex. Elaine, seven at the time, developed a strange virus where she kept suddenly falling asleep, just short of unconsciousness. The pediatrician couldn't figure out what was going on, had me call the gas company to make sure there was no carbon monoxide in the house, and of course I was worried sick. I kept trying to call my husband at the number where he said he would be, but there was no answer.

I have wondered a lot about this incident. Years later when I read John Bradshaw's Family Secrets, I was struck by what he wrote about children somehow picking up clues that something was happening with a parent, could begin having their own symptoms of something wrong, perhaps to draw attention away from a family problem. There seems to be a particular burden for the first-born child that has a father with a destructive secret. Bradshaw writes: "Whatever unresolved emotional baggage the father is carrying, whatever the father is not dealing with openly, the first sibling will often take it on." What I knew years later was that on this trip, my children's father went into one of those massage parlors and paid for sexual contact—the first (at least that he has told me) of many times. All I knew then, and for many years later, was that I had been alone with a sick child and a preschooler and couldn't reach their father.

Right before Elaine had become ill, a publisher had called and offered me a book contract—if I could write that book in three weeks. By the time I reached my husband, Elaine's strange illness had been resolved and I wanted to see if he would support me in this crazy writing venture. And he did.

When I bring out the snapshots of that emerging monster, it is important to express how seldom I or anyone in our daily life saw this monster. When my husband came home, he was concerned about our child and supportive of my work. When the girls were very small, he took care of them most Saturdays so I could write in the back room of our local library. I was grateful then, and I am still grateful now. My daughters tell me that men of their generation do these things now as a matter of course, but then, though there were stay-at-home dads, such help was still somewhat of a novelty.

I think what was difficult was the close to canonization for sainthood this help seemed to earn my husband from his extended family, and even some friends. I was after all making money on these books, all of which went to family income. I was taking care of our girls the other six days of the week.

At some point when they were young, my husband began to refuse to come to church with us on Sundays. What I later learned was that those Sundays were a time for him to watch pornography.

Yet in those days, when I saw that monster appear, it was as if my husband had put on a monster mask that I knew he would soon remove. Those were the times he got right in my face and yelled. Those were the times when he began to pound on the kitchen table when he became angry.

And again, we are back to him angry at me for his shortcomings. One night, I served a dinner with meatballs. I seem to remember cutting up the kids' meatballs into small pieces, or cautioning them to do so, but I cut my own in half. In one bite, that half meatball firmly lodged itself in my throat. I felt it stick, couldn't speak, and knew this was trouble. I stood up from the table, my hands near (but apparently not on) my throat. I am sure it was a shorter period than it seemed, but all I could see was my family just looking at me, and I had visions of the newspaper headlines: "Woman Chokes to Death While Family Keeps Eating."

Finally, remembering the first aid class I had been required to take as a Girl Scout leader, I ran into the bath and rammed myself into the vanity, a sort-of emergency self-Heimlich maneuver. Shaken but breathing, I came back (family still eating) and asked Joseph why he hadn't done the Heimlich when I was choking.

Oblivious I was used to, but the anger surprised me. He pounded on the table, said I hadn't given the universal sign for choking (both hands crossed at the throat) and went upstairs to sulk that I had "accused" him of not helping me.

I sat, stunned at all of this, my throat still hurting, until the girls finished dinner and then went upstairs, wondering how this was my fault. By the time I too went upstairs, and tried to talk to Joseph, his monster mask had slipped away and I mainly saw a petulant child in my husband's face.

Summer, 2010
Survival Snapshot: Day to Day

Day to day, there was the man I loved—the husband and father who helped with dishes and laundry, who laughed with me and our children, who went with me to take kids swimming and to the park. There was the man I made love with and could never imagine not being married to. Friends commented on our strong marriage.

Looking back, I wonder how I missed that growing monster, but for much of our marriage, there were the moments when he put on the monster mask or sank into being a child—and then seemingly those moments were gone.

And who doesn't have moments of being a child—or a monster? My kids still laugh about the time I went berserk because I couldn't find the remote control when the news came on. Our television was set up so that the channels could only be changed through the remote. There I was, jumping and screaming, "I want the remote. I just want to see the news!"

Perhaps the kids' laughter was the difference between silly monster and dangerous monster—and the fact that in another moment, I was laughing at myself as well.

Regardless, I didn't see, during these incidents with my husband when no one was laughing, that the man was disappearing into the monster—child wearing monster mask, monster child, and finally full-grown monster. It took a long time for the mask to become the man.

Ben, the counselor, thought he had us on the right road. We moved, and I desperately hoped this crazy period was over. I hoped the days were over when I had to get to the mailbox before my young children in case there was pornography, which had started to come after that set of

900 calls. I hoped I wouldn't ever again have to put in a Stop order at a post office.

I hoped that in another place, removed from the nearby jump to my in-laws, a town where the traffic was easier and stress was less, that we could pull back together as a couple, as co-parents, and heal.

Summer, 2010
Survival Snapshot: Recognizing Bananas

Healing is not always a straight path, or the path we expect. Sometimes, even death is a form of healing.

After we moved, I found freedom in being away from my mother-in-law's regular contact, freedom in this house surrounded by woods, birds, and the occasional red fox or family of white-tailed deer. Here, I didn't have to cut the grass to a certain length to satisfy a neighborhood association. I entertained as I wanted, mostly kids' parties and increasingly, as my girls grew older, with a circle of teenagers around the table. Writing was going well, and I began to teach writing. And it seemed Joseph was happy—satisfied with me, with home, with work.

But as we were getting older, so of course were our parents. My father-in-law, who had had both a cardiac bypass and throat cancer while we lived nearby, began to increasingly show signs of Alzheimer's disease.

In my husband's family, my father-in-law was my favorite. He (and his whole side of the family) was a bit quieter, easier to get along with, and seemed interested in me beyond just being Joseph's wife. My father-in-law, whose wife nor mother neither drove, was a man used to taking care of others with little complaint. He was handy around the house, planted a garden, and had no meanness in him. When I met my husband's parents when I was twenty-one years old, I thought my husband would age like this father. Joseph had the same tall stature as his dad, some of the same facial features, and to my young eyes seemed to have some of the same mannerisms. Certainly, like his father before him, my husband had learned to just leave the room when his mother and sisters began yelling at each other in the kitchen.

Imagine my horror later, as our marriage matured, when I realized that my husband had aged not like his father, but like his mother, where sarcasm and manipulation reigned. In the end, I was married to my mother-in-law in a man's body, with sexual addiction thrown in—every woman's nightmare!

But back up those years. Even as I began to understand that Joseph had an addiction to pornography and 900 phone calls, I didn't understand that once the sexual addiction monster had its claws in a man, it would not go quietly away once recognized. The monster was only lying dormant, waiting for another chance to grow stronger.

What I did understand was that my father-in-law was growing increasingly worse. Yet my husband's family was firmly rooted in denial. Even my sister-in-law, a clinical psychologist, kept claiming this was depression or something—anything—but what it was. During this time, somehow my mother and father-in-law drove across the state to visit. The minute they got out of the car, I could hear them fighting about getting lost along the way. They came in and settled down a bit and my father-in-law asked if I had any bananas. I pointed towards a bunch on the kitchen counter and went on talking to my mother-in-law. Ten minutes later, I found him wandering around the living room and asked him what he needed. "The bananas," he answered. I took him back into the kitchen and reintroduced him to the bananas, and wondered how in the world he had driven across the state when he could no longer find or always recognize bananas.

Alzheimer's is a cruel disease where the person can be reasonably normal for a day or several days and then not be able to recognize a banana. It was another three-year progression before he died, having developed stomach cancer but not really being able to tell anyone what hurt so that it was not diagnosed until he died blessedly quickly.

But I remember this visit especially well. I wanted to take photos of him then while he was still mostly himself, wanted to show the character (that strange kind of beauty we seem to find so difficult to recognize as people grow older) in his face. I still regret that I didn't get out my old 35mm Pentax and take those portraits. I did take pictures of my husband and his father that Christmas, and later enlarged them as gifts to Joseph and to his mother. We hung Joseph's picture with the family pictures on our wall, but I sent that picture with my husband when he left home.

I have kept three things that were gifts from my father-in-law: a basket that he made, a pair of oak chairs he re-caned, and a little bookcase he made that my husband left behind and that I recently, over five years later, moved into my kitchen to hold cookbooks.

I moved the bookcase where I would see it often because one night I dreamed of my father-in-law across a river. He came towards me and I told him I was glad to see him. "I have been here all along," he told me, "you just had to be ready for contact again."

It is sometimes easier to reconnect, in dreams and in memory, with the dead than the living. Shortly after divorce, I had also dreamed of my father-in-law teaching a school in a garage with old-fashioned school desks. This made waking sense as he once refinished an old school desk for my children. My husband and I were both there and he told us that life is a classroom.

I do not know if Joseph has ever dreamed of his own father. Certainly in the ten years after his father's death when we were still together, he never mentioned any such dreams. I am guessing that he is not ready for contact.

And I wish he could have been open to whatever earthly and heavenly wisdom his father might have passed on. I know that my own father, who died five weeks after our first child was born, was a tremendous source of wisdom to me in my own life and has continued to be a guide in both dreams and memory since.

If those fathers had been able to stay in our lives, or if somehow Joseph had developed that father within to call on for wisdom, would this story be different? Again, I don't know beyond what instinct tells me. I think so.

After Joseph's father died, I saw the scared child emerge more often and the monster begin to grow more powerful. One of my good marriage memories is actually my fortieth birthday, the day we received, thankfully at the end of the day, news of Rob's stomach cancer diagnosis. Our first little dachshund, Newton, had died at age sixteen a couple of months before, holding onto life I have always been convinced until I myself had recovered enough from a brush with death. Mononucleosis had been misdiagnosed six months earlier; I had been given an antibiotic for pneumonia, which combined with the mono, came just short of causing my liver to fail. It was a long, bit-by-bit recovery, during which I wondered if this exhaustion was just what it felt like at forty.

On my birthday, Joseph suggested we go out and drive and look into some of the little country antique shops. He never suggested such a thing, and I was touched. In one shop, we found a picture of a little girl and a brown dachshund. Not having much of a budget, we were surprised when the person in the shop offered it to us for ten dollars. We bought the picture, and it was like having my little dog back for my birthday. Though I have put away all other gifts from my long marriage (beyond books I need), I still have that picture hanging where I first hung it in my, once our, bedroom.

Writing this now, I realize that the picture still holds good memories of a time when the man was still intact, though I am sure now the monster came out of hiding when I didn't see it—still, the man was still in control of the monster before that game of hide and seek turned from a game into a life where the man was losing control.

Within a few weeks of the initial diagnosis, the cancer, finally recognized, was ready to take Rob's life. Still, the family was looking at chemotherapy options. One morning, Joseph received a call from his mother to come. By the time I could get the children to school, Joseph had left for the hospital, six hours away.

I remember the helpless feeling of just sitting in my family room. Should I go to him somehow? Should I take the children out of school? Or did my mother-in-law just want her real children with her?

What I didn't know until years later was that the first thing my husband had done when he flew out that door was to go first to an adult book store to watch a porn film before he could face his family and his father's death.

Even today, I am not sure if the fact that the monster-and-man struggle took another ten years before it tore apart our marriage is a testament to the love in the marriage and family, or to my own blindness and ignorance of the power of sex addiction. I hope it was the first, but the problem with unresolved betrayal is that the one who has been betrayed doubts her own perceptions. It takes a long time, if ever, to regain the confidence in your own instincts and perceptions, your own concept of whether something is valid, your own ability to trust again in love.

When my children were growing up, we used to play a game of roller coaster when driving over bumps and dips in the road. Some dips were little, causing just a giggle from the girls in the back seat. Others were those large hills and dips that made our stomachs lurch, made it feel as if our heart were in our throats, that made us gasp before we returned to the even road.

I had a dream once about my own father, right before I made a switch from writing science books on contract to focus on a long work of fiction. In the dream, I was driving along a road. It was beginning to rain. I crossed a bridge and ahead I could see a town with white-washed buildings. It looked a little like I imagine the missions of the west once looked. The sun was shining. It looked like a good place to rest, but somehow I knew this was not where I should be going. Then, at the end of the bridge, I saw my father. Waiting, he was just waiting there to talk to me. "Oh, Daddy," I said, "I've been going the wrong way."

"It's okay," Dad said, "you know the road goes somewhere. Just turn around and go the other way."

In life, my father once said this when we took a wrong road home from a trip and ended up God knows where. My mother is still annoyed at that "you know the road goes somewhere" comment, but it must have stuck with me in some subconscious corner of my mind because that wisdom was there when I needed it.

In a nearby town I have often walked a labyrinth, knowing if I just keep walking, I will eventually get to the center. But in life, those detours sometimes take so long that we really begin to doubt there is a center to reach. Sometimes, we get close to the center, close enough to glimpse that clover-leaf center, but then the path turns again and we realize we are not really there once again.

With this trinity of metaphors—the roller coaster road dips, the road that goes somewhere, the labyrinth path—there is some metaphor for life that I am trying to reach. Perhaps it is staying on the road in some shape or fashion.

The years after my father-in-law's illness and death until our oldest child left for college were full of little dips that made us giggle and enormous hills and valleys that almost took my breath away.

Summer, 2010
Survival Snapshot: Hitting Mailboxes

I think now that we as a family made the best of that dipping and rising road. At least I think we stayed on the road.

Well, mostly we stayed on the road. These were the years when our children had somehow become teenagers. These were the days when a daughter ran off the road and knocked down a neighbor's mailbox while learning to drive. If I have any advice for parents "teaching" a teen to drive, it is: "Don't eat first, because you are going to feel sick to your stomach, and once you get out of the car, hire a driving instructor." My next piece of advice is to find something to laugh about and if possible, some way to use it. Elaine says that every embarrassing moment in her life has been captured in one of my stories. And I did write about a teen hitting a mailbox in later published fiction. Someday I am going to get one of those sweatshirts that announces: "Watch out—you are in my novel."

The joy of writing fiction is that all of the pain and joy magically transform into characters and plots you can see from just enough distance to get a little more perspective on a life road—ultimately your own life road and that of those you've observed. But if you are lucky, no one recognizes some piece of themselves in the story. Or, if they do, they too laugh. When the story was accepted, I read it to my now grown daughter over the phone and she actually liked it and as usual was my best editor.

The writing, though, in this book—this snapshot writing, this true recollection of my own life—is a different kind of writing than I have done in my over thirty years of writing. This all happened in my own life as I write about it with the exception of name changes to protect the innocent— and not so innocent. There is no fiction in this book. Yet, as I have stressed, it is not fact in the sense that the books I have written on science and nature are fact, where I interview the experts and check my facts at least three times. It is all filtered through my own perspective because though I consulted plenty of ministers, counselors, and books, this is how this marriage, this family, this life affected me—how I perceive it as affecting my family. We all have our filters, rosy and dim, and which one we pull out varies. Time and facts in memory sometimes get switched about. But this is how I see it—how I remember it. I tell my writing students that we can sometimes get closer to the real truth—the heart of how we really feel and see life in fiction. But here I have chosen to write nonfiction—as I see it.

And so, as I see it, we pretty well stayed on the road, even crashing into mailboxes. And, at times, I was afraid of crossing a railroad track in the wrong place and getting hit by a train—a true metaphor for me as this is how my grandfather was killed.

I wonder now if my husband's sexual addiction was under control during those years, or if I was just too busy trying to avoid obvious train crashes that I didn't see the hiding monster.

I don't know. I know that after his father died, Joseph was extremely irritable for at least a year. We took a weekend trip with the girls to Memphis, and stopped in a bookstore. And, yes, anyone who knows me knows I can spend a long time in a bookstore, but everyone seemed content and we were on vacation. When we left, one of the girls mentioned something about wishing she had gotten some book and I turned back to go buy it. And right there, as I hadn't seen happen since I had two-year-olds, my husband started screaming he was tired and wanted to leave right now! I think he pounded something. I am sure he didn't lie down on the floor and kick, though if I were writing fiction, that would be the truth of the heart. We escaped the store, without the book, and to be honest, I am sure I ranted and railed in the privacy of our own car about Joseph's tantrum as we drove to the hotel! I remember they had cookies for the guests at the hotel and that calmed us—both the parents and children—down. Grief, low blood sugar? I put on my coping filter and I think laughed about it all. What I can't remember is if Joseph laughed. I don't think so.

Looking back, I think that when Joseph's father died, some stability he had always counted on for himself, and with which to deal with his mother, had also been lost. This was a time for him to grow up, and while I think there were growth spurts, I think the addiction monster kept pulling him back to an adolescent stage—sometimes to a toddler stage. While he was growing weaker, I think the monster was growing stronger, waiting for its chance to fully emerge.

And at the same time with our girls becoming teenagers, I think I was so busy raising teenagers that I missed truly seeing the teenager my husband was becoming. Though if I had, I don't believe now it would have mattered. My job was as his wife. I think a spouse or partner can bring out the best in the other person. One of our counselors said this influence of me and our children had kept Joseph stable. But it was not my job to raise Joseph from teenager to adult. We can support growth in our friends and partners, but the person can only do the growing himself.

I wonder now if at some crucial time in his own adolescence when a parent still has if some influence, or at least responsibility to help find help, the time was just missed when there could've been help. Again, I can't go back in time. I can only guess.

What I do know is that my teenagers needed guidance and help in these years, and I think—I hope—they were given the tools their dad somehow never acquired.

Summer, 2010
Survival Snapshot: Ice Cream

Even while staying on the road, there were ruts in the road with my teenagers, times when I wondered if we would ever spin our way out of the gravel. I can still hear the pings of gravel making dents in the car.

To me, nothing strikes a mother's sense of wholeness harder than when a child has a problem. There is some mother-sense that kicks in and lets a mom know something is not quite right. The question becomes can she do anything about it.

As heartrending as it has been to lose a husband in every way but a physical body that still resembles the man I knew, I am grateful to have two grown—and wonderful—daughters.

A friend of mine has a grown daughter trapped in alcohol and drug addiction whom I have heard her call a lost daughter. I know that she has tried for many years to help this daughter, but addiction has, at least for now, won the battle. To keep her own sanity, my friend has had to let her daughter loose and pray she someday returns to health.

I have another friend whose son shot and killed schoolmates, and so is in prison. I admire the way she visits this son, but goes on with life beyond this horrible fact—the way she works with other kids in the community, participates in life with her grown daughter, and is still able to laugh. She has even survived breast cancer. During the separation from my husband, I met up with this friend for coffee.

I can still see her with a jaunty pink and brown polka-dot scarf decorating her outfit. I thought then that if she could bring a smile to herself and me with that scarf and share a cup of coffee with me after all she had been through, I too could survive. I could survive losing a husband if she could survive losing a son. It is a hard lesson to learn that no matter how much we love someone, sometimes praying is all that is left for us to do. I remember the anguish for my friend when her son, still a young teen, was suddenly a ward of the prison system. She could not be there to make sure he ate breakfast, wasn't getting a cold—couldn't try to talk to him when there was a possible opening even if he mostly shrugged her off. The night after the shooting, our church held a prayer vigil for all of the children. I took my own children, telling them that sometimes all we can do is pray, but it is important to pray.

But when our children are still home, we keep trying—certainly we keep praying and trying to hear any answers. Actually, I think mothers always do this, but eventually we become more listeners and sometime advisors than actually sneaking pureed broccoli into the meatloaf. And though there were times when I was ready to book a triple room at the state mental hospital for myself and my children, I kept trying, kept praying, kept listening for clues from my kids and answers from God through those teen years. And I am grateful that there was that grace in timing that kept my family together through those years.

I wonder now how emotionally present my husband was even through those years, how often he was leaving his family for a fantasy world where life was just Joseph and some anonymous, large-breasted woman.

I don't know, and have finally accepted that I will never know. What I do know is that there were two parents physically present—perhaps only one and a half emotionally present, but it was enough to help my children, and myself, through their teen years.

Our oldest child began having an increase in stomach, migraine, and biochemical disturbances at puberty. There seemed to be an endless round of doctors and tests, and she is still dealing with keeping all of this in balance.

The combination of this physiology and having a hard time fitting into high school society (I have never seen anyone hate high school so much and love college as much as Elaine) resulted in a full-blown clinical depression during her sophomore year in high school. I had had that mother-sense that something was really wrong for weeks and tried to discuss this with her dad, but he told me I was just worrying over nothing.

I remember Joseph's mother visited during this period and told us that we worried too much, that this worry was like a rocking chair, rocking and rocking, and not going anywhere. Of course, this was the woman who never wanted to pay for counseling for her own kids and told me a mother's job was to keep the house clean. Now, I have nothing against a clean house, but beyond basic cleanliness and safety and food safety (which my children will tell you I am a bit of a fanatic about, having spent too many years looking at microscopic organisms), I never accepted that keeping the house constituted being a good mom. Too many things can happen to kids while you are cleaning the kitchen floor.

Soon after this visit, everything got worse for my girl. I remember praying what I now call a mother's prayer that I hoped then and hope now there is some special forgiveness for a mother's demands. "Okay, God," I prayed, "I need the right help and I need the right help now for my daughter. No fooling around."

The next day, we found an insurance-approved counselor who was available right away. When we went to the office, I expected the experienced counselor whose name was on the office, a woman older than myself, but it was her daughter who was also a counselor that saw my daughter. Had I heard wrongly? It turned out that this was just the right person for my daughter—young enough to relate more fully to her, old enough to also guide me, and most of all kind enough to take the real time and care needed, even calling at times to make sure we got home alright. She was truly an answer to prayer.

Another thing that I learned during this time was to find moments of joy with my children in all situations. Elaine and I drove almost an hour for the counseling sessions and discovered on the way home, an ice cream shop. It eventually became our custom to stop after the counseling for ice cream—just the two of us. A number of years have passed now and while I still remember my own fears for my daughter and doubts about my mothering during that period, I also remember eating that sweet ice cream with my daughter.

I have a picture of Elaine, taken her senior year in high school before a dance. She is smiling, looking radiant in a maroon dress, and has both of her arms held high. She continues to need to take care of her health, and I am so proud of her. I think we were able to give her in those young years the tools to find help when needed.

Lynn had, at least on the surface, an easier time in high school. I have never seen anyone so involved in high school! Talk about being on the road! With band, art club, science club, children's choir, youth group, track, tennis, and community theatre, she was on the go—and kept me on the go as well. I kept boxes of juice and peanut butter crackers in the car, so that she could eat as we raced from a track meet to play practice an hour away, often making it in a half an hour. I can still see her changing in the car as I drove, still trying to explain that if one thing was over at eight o'clock and another started, an hour away, at eight o'clock, this timing didn't really work. Where, when I needed him, was Scotty to beam us up?

But moms try to give each child what she needs, and being involved with different groups and trying lots of different things was what this child needed. So, I stayed on the road.

But of course she, too, had her times that equally worried me as her mom. Another result, or perhaps way of dealing with stress for her, was OCD (obsessive-compulsive disorder). I consulted my by now, on call counselor and psychiatrist on this, but was told it was a sign of being conscientious and not to push her on it. I did though try to leave the lines of communication open for her. I remember after one of her close friends died in a car accident at only fifteen how she sat one night and told me she was worried she hadn't done everything just right in an evening ritual to keep everyone she loved safe.

So, again, with my own daughter, I was trying to explain that lesson I struggled so hard to learn myself: we just can't humanly control everything. As I later read in Rabbi Harold S. Kushner's book, <u>When Bad</u>

<u>Things Happen to Good People</u>, I wonder myself if once certain natural laws are set in place if even God can change certain events. I do believe God is available to help us and perhaps, as I have said earlier, to bend time a bit—or at least what we perceive as linear time. But now I am drifting off into a different book—a time fantasy I have been planning to write for years. The old writer's saw is that life gets in the way of publication. I think now that life just switches projects around and the good news is that each book is richer for the life events and the writing that comes from surviving life. But back to safety in everyday time, I don't know if I helped my daughter that evening we talked about the death of her friend, but I do know I was able to put my arm around her, to let her curl up against me as she did as a little girl. Ten years later, we met up at Gail's home, my best friend from high school, to attend a wedding. When Lynn came in from the long drive, she came in and sat for a moment in my lap and leaned against me while I again put both arms around her. She was tired and a little bit later than expected, and I was relieved that she was safe.

Summer, 2010
Survival Snapshot: Grandmother's Bed

When we cross the street, my eighty-three-year-old mom reaches for my hand. Sometimes it is because she needs my support, yet other times I am sure she is remembering me at age six and still trying to keep me safe when crossing the road.

When I sleep now, alone, in my grandmother's bed that I shared with my husband for many years, I remember how I once envisioned a circle of safety when I dropped into bed at night beside him. He was often asleep by the time I came to bed, but when my children had settled for the night and our little dachshund Wilbur was asleep in his dog bed, snoring those soft dog snores, I felt for that moment that my little family was safe.

And for those moments they were, and I think now this is all we can do as mothers—make sure our children are safe moment to moment and leave the rest to God. And the safety I felt with my husband? Whether that was real, I don't know to this day. It is real that he was in that bed next to me, that we kept making a life together with our family, certainly real that I loved him; but what was in his heart and mind? I question now. I think this is a haunting question for most women who have been betrayed: Who was that masked man? Will the real man please stand up?

Perhaps it is best to accept those moments at face value, even while now realizing that Joseph could be in bed next to me and plan for the possibility of seeing other women. Perhaps he lied to himself and just thought he would drive by the massage parlor and not go in again, or just get online and see who was there and never meet anyone again. Again, I don't know, and must accept that I will never know.

Even now, in the recent mediation, my now ex-husband exclaimed several times when certain obligations or promises were recalled, "I don't remember that—at all!" The mediator points to what is written in black and white. Even now, I wonder, as I did when the worst of our marriage trouble finally came to light, if this is some early sign of the Alzheimer's disease that took his father's mind, or some deterioration of the frontal lobe of the brain from the vascular damage of diabetes. I do think these are possibilities—that these things could be working on his mind to weaken the impulse control that once fought the addiction. Yet all still comes back to the addiction monster itself taking over as much control as possible—certainly any influence I ever had. I begged my husband to get a full work-up, to go to a clinic that specialized in sex addiction to have the physiological tests, the psychological counseling—to really find every opportunity for healing. He refused. "Do you know what that would cost?" he asked.

That old family pattern, from what I have learned, is officially his "family of origin" of not being willing to pay for healing, but eternally paying for the aftermath of avoidance was back again. I remember asking in return if he had any idea of what a divorce would cost both of us. I meant in more than money, but he replied that he didn't need much. And so now, I find myself facing a man angry at me for what divorce has financially cost who won't, or can't, remember agreeing to any responsibility "at all."

And because account statements are what I can use in court, I present my lawyer with all of those financial costs of surviving and making sure my children survived as well as possible, post divorce—of the remaining portion of the family home mortgage which Joseph agreed to pay off and now feels is unfair (and so wants me forced into selling my home), of the girls' tuition bills that I paid though he had agreed to pay a portion, of the life insurance we took out when we were first married and I have paid until now—all those bits and pieces of our history—a history that he is now trying to rewrite. And of course we each have our own version of history—and I find now, that at least it seems in a no-fault state, that the only history that counts in court is the history recorded in written receipts and signed documents.

These accounts, according to my lawyer, are all to my advantage in this battle I never wanted to fight. Being the one in the marriage that did the record-keeping, that drafted the initial separation agreement with his complete agreement because my husband was more interested then in adding "separated" to his dating profile than in being bothered with such matters, I am the one with the financial records—with what essentially now is the record of historical treaties (three of them), also known as divorce agreements and amendments, that we have signed over the last seven years. These are what my lawyer will present to the judge while I, I hope, can sit calmly by and pray that at least those documents in writing will be upheld by human legal judges. I do not want money back for tuition or other unpaid expenses, I want only to defend my home.

But finances are not the real cost to our lives, at least to my life, since I do remember the rest of the history.

When I was a child, there was a drama called "Divorce Court" — not one of the actual reality shows so popular now, but a drama acted from what I suppose might have been real cases. Once, while staying with my grandmother, I saw the show on her old black and white TV. I remember that it was about infidelity, in this case a man who thought his wife had been unfaithful. The climax of the show came when it was announced with a preamble of music that a doctor had now determined that the husband had been rendered sterile during the war and therefore the child of the marriage could not possibly be his. The music boomed, the man looked crestfallen, but the case was clearly solved with the unfaithful wife being soundly condemned. This was obviously before the days of no-fault divorces. I do not know all of the legal reasons for the changes in laws, though I am sure some are valid. What I remember, though, taking away from this drama I saw in childhood, was that infidelity in a marriage was not without consequences to anyone—the mother who could lose the child, the crestfallen man, the child who had just lost the security of knowing that the man she thought of as her father was not her biological father and the mother that she thought she knew had betrayed that loved father. The little drama had made its point to me: everyone was supposed to be faithful in a marriage and if not, this would come out in public to resounding music.

This might be one basis for those no-fault laws—divorce is hard enough on people and especially on children—without that music. But I think we have somewhere lost the knowledge that the betrayed spouse is crestfallen and he or she is a long time climbing out of that valley, especially if the betrayer somehow rewrites history in his or her mind and keeps claiming he or she is now suddenly the victim. This need to reverse history seems especially true of addicts, and I do think addicts become victims of their own addictions. But this was the path they started down, not the path their partner pushed them down; and in my case, I did everything I could to give my husband a hand off of that addiction road—a hand pushed away in no uncertain terms. And it is that history that I must share here because that can no longer, as in that old black and white drama, be presented in court to resounding music.

It is that history I live with when I get into bed at night, still in what was once my grandmother's bed and once was once our marriage bed. When my husband finally told me that yes, he had been intimate with other women, had paid them and "let them" touch him, we were sitting in the car in the parking lot of the school where our daughters had gone to high school, from which our youngest would be graduating in another couple of months.

Three days earlier, with Elaine home on spring break from college, we were all four getting ready to go to a zoo in a nearby city for a family outing. I had told Joseph that I thought there was something going on that he had not told me. I had earlier in the new year taken Lynn to visit a college. She and I had gotten caught in an unexpected ice storm and had to stay a couple of days. Since then, I had sensed that Joseph, who had been doing so well in therapy, had relapsed into pornography addiction or worse. He had denied any relapse until that morning. I am still amazed that he told me, "Yes, there is more, but not much." It was early in the morning and I was still lying on the bed. And somehow I knew that this "not much" was going to make a big difference in my life, in his life, in our family's life. I remember a weakness holding me on the bed, a weakness that I had never felt before—it seemed that all of the strength suddenly drained from my body. I wondered if I could get up. But then my bowels turned to water and I was forced to get up and run to the bathroom. Somehow we went on to the zoo that day with our girls. It was the last time we were fully a family.

When Elaine then left to go back to college, I insisted we drive somewhere away from where Lynn could hear and he tell me what "not much" meant. And so there we sat in the parking lot. There was no resounding music, but I am sure I looked crestfallen. I had about convinced myself Joseph was "just" participating in cybersex or something again that didn't involve someone off the screen—and that, I thought then, though I wonder now, was something I still thought therapy could see us through. But knowing that my husband had physically walked into places with sex for sale, even wearing the wedding ring I had given him over twenty-five years ago, was different. Not to mention the emotional breaking of my heart, these betrayals could have endangered my very life with the possibility of HIV and other sexually transmitted diseases. His sex addiction no longer fell into the "we're all still trying to figure out what to do with all of this porn now on the Internet, and what's okay in marriage and what isn't category." I remember the shock, how I said in what would've made a great scene in the old "Divorce Court" show, "But that's adultery." My purse was open and I grabbed my keys and slapped him across the face with them. This probably wasn't the best response, but I can't say I regret it. I am glad it wasn't a gun in my purse, and it did show me that I needed to be careful with the way I controlled my own pain.

Months later, when we sat in another car in our own driveway to discuss more, I had had the forethought to put the car keys on the front porch. My husband, by now living in his own apartment, was coming over to discuss some of the things that had happened. I had by now realized he was seeing another woman, perhaps other women. I remembered a case about a betrayed woman who had run over her cheating husband and killed him. The earlier incident with the car keys had shown me that this kind of hurt could make me irrational. Though my biggest response to even anger is uncontrollable tears, I really didn't trust myself with a whole car.

In the discussion, I learned the other woman was young with small children, and also married. And he claimed to see nothing wrong with this. I got out of the car. I was glad then for the keys on the porch, but when he angrily reached for the door to get out of the car, something triggered the panic button and the locks started going up and down, the panic button blaring, and he was trapped. I had never had this happen before (and never have since), but in a moment, I realized that I needed the keys to stop the panic reaction in the car. I ran to get the keys and I have always thought that this was just a little gift of humor from God, or the guardian angel that hovers around weeping wives, because the stunned panic on Joseph's face was priceless. I guess he thought I had rigged the car to blow up, especially when I sprinted away. I got the keys and pressed the button. He scrambled out of the car and into his car—and I have never seen a man leave so quickly!

But this was months later after the initial confession. Back in that earlier March, he was driving the car, and took us home. I remember we went into our bedroom and he began to get changed for bed. But I was never going to feel that circle of safety and security with him again. I didn't know that fully then, but I remember suddenly saying, "No, not in my grandmother's bed, not in my grandmother's bed."

I had never really thought so much of the bed before as primarily my grandmother's bed—it was our bed, along with so many things we kept inheriting. (I really only remember buying one main piece of furniture together during our marriage—a kitchen table we paid on week by week.) But in that moment, I knew how incensed she would be at him climbing back into bed as if he had just admitted he'd spent a few extra dollars on cookies the doctor had told him not to eat, rather than admitting he had paid for sex.

My little Southern Baptist grandmother, married herself at fifteen, was not of a generation that tried for political correctness. She would've called a spade, a spade; an adulterer, an adulterer. And though I think even she would've counseled trying to heal the marriage, the forgiveness I have tried—day by day—to keep doing before and since divorce, it was her spirit of survival, of standing up for oneself that I needed in that moment and have needed since.

I couldn't physically imagine the man who had just admitted he had cheated, taken family money to do so, and lied to me for I still don't know how many years, lying beside me again in my grandmother's bed. That circle of security was broken. As I tried to still work over the next months with my husband, I had plans for putting Grandmother's bed in another bedroom and buying us a new bed to start over. But my husband wanted his own apartment, his own bed.

And so now I sleep alone in my grandmother's bed. I have slept with dogs and cats since, and imagine I will again when I find it in my heart to adopt a new pet. Sometimes, my youngest daughter crawls up in her great-grandmother's bed when she is home as she once did when she was a little girl, so we can just talk in the early morning or late at night. I am grateful for the moments now and even for the good memories. Once, our girls crawled up in bed on early mornings between their father and me, and we said we were a sandwich. "A peanut butter sandwich?" "A cheese sandwich?" "A family sandwich," I would answer. I hope these memories still hold warmth for my girls.

I cannot present this statement of the real cost of betrayal and divorce in black and white statements of numbers and legal documents. This is why I am taking the time to write in words because the real cost of addiction, betrayal, and divorce has little to do with numbers.

Midsummer, 2010
Survival Snapshot: Mountains

Now, it is June—the month when finally all of the numbers and agreements are once again examined by a judge. "Two weeks. I turned the calendar page," Mom said. "We go to court this month and I can't wait."

I feel myself smile weakly, knowing she is thrilled at another chance to glare at my ex-husband, this time where he can't hide from her. But I am touched by the "we." When I was a girl, Mom would show guests my latest sewing projects and say, "Look what we made," even though she couldn't read a pattern. Though especially true between mothers and daughters, with anyone we love there is a "we" component to our accomplishments and challenges. When we have helped a child, a friend, a spouse, even an organization to create or cope in any way, there is some community that forms. I think this is a good thing. I also think when that "we," for a couple, for a family, and even for the extended community of family and friends that the couple was a part of, is split apart by divorce. Divorce is rarely such a clean break as we want to think. Mom refers to death as a cleaner break than divorce, and while we still struggle to resolve old arguments at new times in our lives with the dead, at least they can't force us to court!

When I told a writer friend that I had put aside my almost-finished (of course, it has been almost finished now for about five years) novel in order to write a book about this marriage, this divorce, this long aftermath, she said, "That's one way of getting even." I laughed, but at the same time I was protesting that it really wasn't about getting even. I hope not. "But it might help a lot of people," she added. I hope so. Writing has always helped me understand my own life better and I hope some of this flows over into other people's solutions as well, as reading about other lives—sometimes on the surface having little to do with mine—has helped me. It is usually the survival I take away from someone's story.

I explained to my friend about how I had realized the book was about the effects of one partner's addiction on his spouse and on a family, but more fully, it was about how I had survived betrayal and divorce, was still surviving betrayal, and how my girls and I had survived as a family as we each grew into our new lives. New lives though are built on old lives. In this sense, maybe I am writing to "get even"—not though to get back at anyone, but just to even out my old life in order to keep going forward.

My first job out of college was to help raise tobacco "worms" from egg to each of the five stages of caterpillar growth to pupae stage to moth—and then the cycle would start again. Two different scientists I worked for were studying these animals and their large, slowly dividing cells, to do medical research. Different stages of growth were needed for different studies, but what I remembered after that conversation with my writer friend was how carefully I had to turn those pupa throughout their maturing time so that all stayed even—otherwise the moth that finally emerged wouldn't be strong on both sides, might not even survive, and then that cycle of growth would have been stopped.

So, for myself, for my daughters, and for anyone that might take away any insight or skill, I have been going back into those small, dark boxes and turning the memories this way and that until they nestle into an even time until the next time I need to turn them again.

Now, the time that has come back to my mind is the two and a half year period of time before Joseph made what I think of as his "women of the flesh" confession in the high school parking lot. During that blessed time, it truly seemed as if all of the therapy, all of the effort, all of the love had worked in our marriage. I am still grateful for that time when my husband and I talked and laughed, and looked forward to our empty nest. Elaine was in college and we were beginning to look with Lynn for colleges. I saw Joseph relax without that constant burden of addiction riding on his back, saw him take the time to actually make Christmas ornaments for children at work, take the time to talk with me, be willing to browse at least a little in life. He laughed and smiled more. Friends and family commented on how happy he seemed. It was not an easy road getting to that point, but I thought once he was on it, surely he would want to keep traveling that good road.

This good stretch of road started with another addiction pothole to be repaired. One evening, after Elaine was in college, I came home from taking Lynn to community play practice and ran into the downstairs bathroom. Like some nightmare dream that keeps recycling through my mind, I saw the room covered with pornographic pictures printed off the computer. My first thought was to grab them up, glad I had gone in this room before my daughter. My second was to stumble up the stairs and hold them up to my husband. I will never forget how shocked Joseph himself looked—shocked that he had left them out, or just how fully the addict was in control, I don't know. I can't even remember now the sequence of this time, only that at first he denied they were his. Since neither our daughter nor I had put them up and the dog and cat couldn't operate a computer or tape things on a wall, Joseph finally had to admit that yes, they were his. He kept insisting it was just the change in our lives, the stress at work—this was a one-time recurrence. On the surface of my mind, I think I believed this, but the time ten years earlier when I had had to screen the mail, the bills, the phone—protect my children and my own heart—came rushing back.

I insisted he get some help for this stress or whatever it was, got a stack of books from the library with such titles as When to Leave, and prayed. I talked, with my husband's encouragement, to the closest of friends, one of my ministers, and I went on with getting our youngest daughter to all of her high school activities and talking with our oldest child often as she adjusted to college.

Eventually, Joseph admitted that this had not been the first time his "problem" had recurred, but insisted again there had been no physical contact with other women. Why did this make such a difference? First, there were the health concerns, and second, I was just beginning to understand then the stages of addiction—how one leads to another, especially with the technology that leads someone from the picture to a person (though probably not the one in the perfect picture). He didn't fool just me, but the counselor and even a lie detector test the counselor had him take regularly: a technique in treating sex addicts to keep them honest with themselves and everyone else. But someone so divided that they lie to themselves is not, I learned, a very reliable truth teller to even a machine.

Still, though I dreaded the times when he would go off to the sexaholics meetings (SA, built on the same principles as AA) as a reminder of this intrusion in our seemingly normal lives, this all seemed to be working for him. When Lynn asked where Dad went on Tuesday nights, I said he was at a meeting with other men where they were all trying to help each other be better men. And I think they were—for a time.

Joseph felt good about himself, about his sobriety, and I saw him really work on becoming a better man—a happier man. We celebrated our twenty-fifth wedding anniversary.

It is surprisingly difficult to write anything about that twenty-fifth anniversary. It was a good time. So it is difficult now, knowing what came after, to recapture that feeling of joy. It is a little like watching a movie for the second time, knowing during the love scene that disaster will be coming in the next scene. You want to freeze the frame of time right there for those characters, but then you wouldn't really understand the story.

Joseph wanted to take a small trip to celebrate the anniversary, so we went to the Ozarks, stayed in a bed and breakfast, explored the area.

The picture that I would ask time to stand still for, if even for just this page, is of that couple standing on an Arkansas bluff overlooking the Big Bear River. He turns to her, with a real smile—one of joy—and holds out his arms. She goes willingly into that embrace. They have made it twenty-five years, they have come through the problems—this marriage will endure.

But then they have to come down from the mountain.

Midsummer, 2010
Survival Snapshot: Levels of Hell

I have seen in all kinds of addicts—drug, alcohol, sex—a tendency to counterbalance any moment of great happiness with an equally great effort to spoil the fruits that happiness could bring. Within months, if not days, of getting a job or a chance at a job, of real relationship, or having climbed any hill in life, an addict will stand at the edge of that hill and hurl himself off. Those who love him (or her) can't stand on the hill, enjoying the view—they can only try to keep their foothold as they trudge down the hill to see how bad the damage, and then she (or he) starts back up the hill on her own.

The addict's tumble off the hill seems to me (I have no studies, no statistics here—just observation) to come within two to three years of sobriety. Sometimes the addict can begin trudging back up the hill and build along the way, perhaps taking steps higher or even an occasional step down, but still with their feet firmly planted towards life and relationships—towards all of the support of those who stood by them while they made their way out of Hell. I know this success happens. Yet I also know how often the addict has not just a lapse, but takes a leap back down into Hell. And if we put levels of Hell into this metaphor, I think a relapsing addict tends to land in a deeper level of Hell than ever.

There are then fewer hands reaching out, but even those still reaching can't seem to grasp their loved one in that underworld. Life has become innumerably more difficult.

There are many world myths where someone among the living goes into the underworld to bring someone they have loved back to the life they have lived together. But it rarely works. In some versions, the living one cannot resist looking back at their loved one and the beloved sinks back into death, or as in one Cherokee story, becomes a red cardinal rather than the loved human. The only myths where the dead return wholly to the living are those where the dead loved one finds some strength within to return to the living. In those myths, there are often helpers, certainly the living are taking care of matters above world that will make it possible for the dead to return. They are constantly petitioning for divine help, but it becomes clear in myth after myth that no matter how great the love, the living cannot restore the dead to life alone—and that in some way the dead have to want to do the work to live—have to find the necessary strength of being stripped down and cleansed, of accepting life without the addiction, to emerge from the tomb.

I know this happens, but I am afraid it is much rarer than I once believed. People talk about hitting rock bottom, but I don't know where rock bottom finally is for some people. It seems a long way down.

For my husband, sitting in the parking lot of his daughter's high school, telling his wife of then twenty-six years that while she had taken their child for a college audition—through a late February ice storm—he had withdrawn money from their savings to buy a pornography movie and then had visited a place called "The Playplace" to "play" with another woman was not the bottom. Confessing to me that this was not the first time was not the bottom.

Midsummer, 2010
Survival Snapshot: Flying into Glass

When I read those library books about when to leave, one bit of advice that stuck with me was determining: What is your bottom line? What line in the sand is the one that once your partner walks across it is finally the last line left?

From the outside looking in, I think it is difficult to know why a partner of someone that has betrayed her (or him) is still standing at least nearby the betrayer. I know those who love me, my family and friends, and sometimes perhaps even my own children, wondered if I would ever find that bottom line. We have all watched the press conferences where the wife of some prominent man is standing near him with the frozen, shocked look on her face while he makes a public confession. We have all wondered, why she is standing there—what is wrong with her?

Whether a woman stands with her man in front of the cameras, or not; whether she eventually stays and we hope he gets it together if she does, or not; or whether the partner doesn't have to face television but just her neighbors without bursting into tears, that shock is the key to why she is standing there at all. She can't yet see another place to go. After years of hope and trying to believe in her partner, it is difficult to even see the sand, not to mention any line in the sand.

Just this weekend, one of the members of the red-tailed hawk family flew from the swing set perch into the middle of the yard. As I watched from the kitchen window, the hawk headed straight towards my back, glass doors. I was sure the bird would turn before hitting the glass, but it didn't. Fortunately, the hawk did swerve after its first brush with the glass and flew off safely.

I assumed at first this was the young hawk, still learning to navigate a landscape that has not only mice and grasshoppers, but glass doors with confusing sheens and reflections. But now, I wonder. It could have been the father hawk, the male partner of the bonded pair, in some hawk midlife crisis that had been developing for years, having finally lost his bearings completely.

Or it could also have been the mother hawk, the female partner of the pair, in some kind of life shock, only able to see enough ahead to take one flap of the wings at a time, no longer sure of the air beneath her wings or of the reflections of the world around her. Perhaps even in existing in a world of air, she feels that she is drowning—as though she has somehow been pushed under water and is moving in slow motion, hoping if she just keeps moving that reflection of surface will bring her back to where she can breathe. Perhaps she hasn't been able to eat except when some friend hawk calls to her across the wind that she must eat something. Perhaps she hasn't been able to really sleep without nightmares of every nest she has built being swept away. Perhaps she is shivering with an internal cold regardless of the sunshine. Perhaps she is having trouble believing there is any sun, any warmth, left in her world. Perhaps she still has some hawk mother job to complete and she is petrified that she will fail her young.

These were my days after my husband's parking lot confession. I forced myself to drink soy milk while I journaled, usually stopping to answer the phone and talk to my mother or a concerned friend checking to see that I was eating and sleeping. In a daze, I walked downstairs to my basement office and critiqued my writing students' manuscripts and desperately hoped I was making sense about sentence structure, point of view, and when to start a paragraph. I picked my daughter up from tennis practice and drove through somewhere to get us something to eat. I shivered uncontrollably and I could barely keep from crying. I took to wearing sunglasses in the grocery and used the drive-through window at the local drugstore where I had shopped for years and was known by name. I was afraid to say anything to a casual acquaintance for fear the whole story would just pop out of my mouth. I didn't know who realized the trouble in my marriage and who didn't. I hoped somehow I would wake up and find this had all been a terrible nightmare.

After a week on driving through fast food places instead of our usual family dinners, of her father disappearing downstairs, Lynn finally asked, "So, are you going to tell me what is going on?"

I took a breath and said, "Dad's cheated on me."

When she was a couple of years younger, she had asked me once when we passed a "gentleman's club," what those places were. I told her they were places some men went to look at and sometimes touch women they didn't know. She looked at me, totally baffled, and asked, "Why would they want to do that?" I told her I didn't really know.

Now, I had to tell her that her own dad was addicted to such places, and to other sexual encounters with women who were not her mother. And I didn't really know why, except I thought it was like an illness. (I didn't know then and I don't know now if there were any actual affairs while Joseph and I lived together as husband and wife, though I have learned bits of information that make me now think that affairs too became part of the mix, along with one-night stands with women met on the Internet. I know such a one-night stand happened within the first week we actually separated, so Joseph certainly seemed all set up for any and all forms of adultery.)

"Don't tell me," my daughter said, "that those meetings he goes to are like AA." I nodded. "Don't tell me," she said, "they are called SA." I nodded again.

Midsummer, 2010
Survival Snapshot: Stopping and Starting

In this blur of days, when I could find a space where I wasn't crying (I did learn I could do a lot while crying: drive a car, do the dishes, critique students, send out a manuscript), I tried to live with betrayal and to, well, live. I found a way to tell Elaine at college about Dad's addiction, and agreed with Joseph to again try couples counseling. We made plans to go up and see Elaine's college piano recital, where we needed also to host a small reception. I got cupcakes together for the tennis team and friends together for a surprise dinner for our Lynn's eighteenth birthday and tried to think how to get through her high school graduation ceremony, complete with in-laws, the next month. I think I barely missed and probably brushed a number of glass doors during this time, but I kept going.

Even though Joseph pleaded with me to try yet another counselor, once we got there, he was alternately repentant and angry. He didn't want to do the exercises she suggested, but when he did do them, he told her they helped. I was back again on that beastly roller coaster that kept starting and stopping and yet I couldn't find a way off. One minute he was saying how much he loved me and the next that he wanted to see who was out there. To be fair, I did my share of screaming while on the roller coaster!

Midsummer, 2010
Survival Snapshot: Holding Up

During the time of trying to keep my balance in spite of glass doors and roller coasters, the one goal I could see ahead to was giving my last chick a fair sendoff out of the nest. She would only graduate from high school once. Lynn said she wanted "an aunt" there (one of my husband's two sisters) as an aunt had been at her sister's graduation. And so we kept on with plans for Joseph's mother and sister, with her husband and child, to come. I insisted though that Joseph explain to his family that we were having problems. He wanted to have his family still stay at our house while he slept on the floor in our bedroom and me pretend all was fine—I suppose also fixing chicken casserole. But I couldn't pretend all was fine. Now, that I knew the whole truth (or at least a lot of the whole truth), I wasn't going to lie to myself and everyone else.

The in-laws stayed in a motel and we planned a dinner at a local restaurant. Thank God for friends. The only way I kept myself together and found some joy in Lynn's graduation was with the help of friends.

My mother-in-law was mad at my husband, pouting at the schedule when it didn't work for her; my sister-in-law, who told me I would always be her sister (Joseph says his sister is now encouraging him to try to change the agreement and take my home five years after this had been settled), somehow talked me into keeping her five-year-old daughter overnight to "stay with her cousin." Of course, my daughter, the cousin, was sleeping in the next morning after the all-night Project Graduation. Though I had also been up all night helping with Project Graduation, I found myself up with my niece the next morning making teddy bear pancakes and playing princess. I am though in an odd way glad for that time with the little girl. Being an only child, I was thrilled to finally be an aunt when my sister-in-law and her husband adopted. I had even agreed to serve as guardian with Joseph should anything happen to the parents. Then, everything collapsed with my husband. And though I tried to send cards and gifts after the divorce, I finally realized her mother no longer considered me a sister, so my attempts to reach out would only be confusing to the child. Aunt Who?

So, what kept me at least standing through Lynn's graduation were dear friends. An older couple that had been honorary grandparents for my children for a number of years, who were dear friends of ours and still of mine, came to the dinner. And my friend, Marie, one of the true sisters of my heart was able to come. I have a picture of Marie and me before the graduation dinner, me wearing ridiculously high heels that she and I had gone shopping for on a lark. In this picture, she is keeping me from falling as we pose, her in her sensible Birkenstocks, me in those silly heels. I am so grateful for that memory, for her being there to hold me up. This sister of my heart was then in a brief remission from a recurrence of breast cancer that had metastasized into her intestines. Within a short time after the graduation, Marie's cancer returned in force and it would be me— physically at least—holding her up as I traveled to her home to help her with chemotherapy treatments, liquid feedings, living until she died, and finally, some acceptance of death.

My mom repeats as a rule of fate that things come in threes. I laugh about this when she says it, but as usual moms are often right. The nest was emptying, my marriage was collapsing, and my best friend was dying.

Midsummer, 2010
Survival Snapshot: Vanilla Nectar for Hummingbirds

The juxtaposition of Marie dying from breast cancer while desperately wanting to live and my husband relentlessly destroying the life we had built together while telling me what he wanted was "big breasts" was a crazy parallel that would never have occurred to me in fiction. There are still times I have a hard time believing it was reality. To make matters crazier, as Marie pointed out, I even have large breasts!

At one point during all of this time, after six months of counseling, my husband and I decided to try a little trip together—the counselor assuring us we were making such good progress. The trip went reasonably well, but as I had finally learned, any up with my husband had come to precede a gut-wrenching plunge where the addict monster emerged, rested and ready to take charge. A few days after we got back in town, we had gone up to a nearby city for dinner; encouraged by the counselor, I thought maybe we could build on this tiny island of harmony. On the ride home, I suggested we make love when we got home. During the preceding months, a coldness had come over my husband at the mention of any marital intimacy, and I saw that coldness come over him then. He mumbled something about allergies. Eternal optimist that I tend to be, I pressed on with, "Well, maybe there is something you want that I can do." I had some thought of silk sheets or a blond wig, or I don't know what, but he answered, "I want big breasts."

"But I have big breasts," I said.

"I don't want them saggy," he said.

I don't know if a man understands this hurt, but I think any woman reading this will know that such a comment from a man you have been married to for over twenty-five years, to whom you have born two children, who you thought would love you through time, will know that it felt as if he had just punched me in the stomach.

Intellectually, I can see now that such cruelty was part of his own fear of aging, but he had hurt me—and the biggest revelation that evening was that if he found a weak spot that hurt me, he would keep punching. Even now, at any perceived weakness—even kindness towards him—Joseph will use that opening as a way to punch at me. As hard as it is for me, I am learning to keep a long, businesslike distance with the being that has now taken over the husband I once adored and raised a family with and planned to spend my life loving.

But then, still stunned, tears starting, I sat there wondering when he had become so mean, when he added, "And you have gained a few pounds over the years! Haven't you?"

And I was stunned again. When our oldest daughter started looking at colleges, I had begun going to Weight Watchers, wanting to be able to keep up with all of the college visiting and hoping to get myself in better shape for life without twenty-four-hour-a-day mothering. I had lost close to forty pounds, and friends and relatives were full of compliments—all but my husband. He insisted he really couldn't see much difference and complained about the fees and was very annoyed when I bought any new clothes, though mostly I bought anything for myself at a consignment shop.

After discovering the porn left in the bathroom after Elaine left for school, I know I lost some motivation for staying in shape. A middle-aged woman literally facing her husband's youthful fantasies posted on the wall finds it discouraging to maintain her own sexiness. The weight began to creep back on. It is true that you need to lose weight and keep it off for yourself. In my case, weight lost or weight gained was only a weapon with my husband to blame me for something. By this scene, Lynn had also left home, Joseph had lost more control of real life, and I wondered: Who was this man next to me in the car?

During this ironic time, Marie's home—even with the bags of nutrients that looked like heavy baby formula in the refrigerator, the smell of the alcohol used to clean the port for medicine and nutrients—with its strange combination of hope and finality with every doctor's visit, was for me some refuge.

I knew her kitchen like I knew my own, and in the chaos of her husband getting ready for work and her teenaged son rushing to high school, there was a familiar comfort that I seemed to be losing in my own home. Though I had tried to do some cooking again for my husband, he didn't appreciate those efforts anymore. He hated to do any cooking himself, though he once announced to me that if we weren't together he would have the whole frozen food section to choose from.

But at Marie's, I was needed. Someone who can just load the dishwasher, hang up a load of laundry, or run to the store is greatly needed in a household where the mother is dying with cancer.

One of the few things Marie could still eat was Cream of Wheat. She said I made it like her mother did—just right. I think now the common technique her mother and I shared in making that Cream of Wheat for her was simply love. The other vital ingredient was her ability to receive that love.

I miss her every day. I miss that kitchen where someone else now lives. And I have learned something sadly amazing—being close to someone who has died, but who was in communion with you in life until the end of this plane of life, is far easier to remain close to than someone still living who has broken faith with you. Recently, I talked again with my friend whose daughter is addicted to alcohol. "Loving someone with an addiction," I said, "is worse than someone dying. Addiction is a living death."

"Exactly," she answered.

For years, Marie and I made a ritual of who would see the first ruby-throated hummingbird arriving in the spring. She always called me first after having seen the first hummingbird. I suspect this is because she always thought to put her feeders out first. She swore though that it was her magic formula of her homemade vanilla sugar that she used to make her nectar.

On my kitchen window, I still keep a little container of that vanilla sugar that she gave me. It is in one of those charming British covered cups decorated with birds. This one is painted with a tufted titmouse, but the sugar is for the hummingbirds. We were in her kitchen when I commented on the two little containers on her counter. She handed me one and said, "One for you and one for me." I make my nectar with plain sugar. Somehow though, her small container of vanilla sugar in my kitchen feels as blessed to me as communion bread. It is not really the taste that matters in such communion food, it is the act of faith that no matter what is happening at the moment, there is a divinity that too has suffered and will help us keep journeying through our own life.

Midsummer, 2010
Survival Snapshot: Forks and Spoons

Part of moving through life's transitions, of adjusting to a loved one no longer physically present due to death or divorce, is rearranging the physical mementoes left behind. There is a ritual of sorting, claiming, cleaning, and then reclaiming those symbols of life that give me a sense of comfort or inspiration in which I have engaged throughout my life. I have, though reluctantly, even learned to discard things that no longer hold true for me as comfort or inspiration.

I suspect some of this desire for comfort around me (in my case, mostly books, handcrafts, photos and greeting cards) is to some degree genetic. My recently married daughter told me that her new husband was becoming a bit overwhelmed with her propensity, too, to accumulate books and those clothes from the thrift stores that she wears so truly well. I commented that it often seemed that a stuff person ended up paired with a non-stuff person. She said that was probably a good thing that led to some balance, where home was neither too overloaded nor too stark.

Certainly, as she is the stuff person in her marriage, I was in mine, as was my father in his—at least in his second marriage. My mom is actually my stepmother. She became my mother when I was four and she married my father, a young widower. She is the mother who took care of me when I was sick, who took me to the swimming pool, who read Charlotte's Web to me. She is in all senses my mother. Now, as she said recently to me, "We are the ones that are taking care of each other."

Yet there was another mother, before Mom, who gave birth to me and, according to all that I have been told, desperately wanted me. In pictures and in the comments of relatives, it is easy to see her gifts of inheritance in my dark eyes and the way my hair curls. I can hear that same family laugh when I talk to my aunt and cousins—I can hear it from my own children. My aunt told me that this mother of mine liked to write.

This mother, who was informed that she could not have children, who conceived after nine years of marriage, committed suicide when I was seven months old. She had what we now call postpartum psychosis. I do not really know the treatments administered over fifty years ago, though I know there is more recognition now of the hormonal problems that can develop after birth. This is a condition that can still take young women's lives, but at least there is more awareness that what can often be dismissed as "the baby blues" can turn deadly. And there is less shame today in suicide itself. We recognize depression as a disease, not a lack of willpower or character. With the knowledge of the day, my father tried to get the best treatment possible for my mother. I know she was institutionalized and, on a brief visit home, jumped from a high rise window while my father went to get the car. I know that my grandmother, my father's mother, was trying to hold onto her when this happened.

And now I know that my grandmother took care of me until my father remarried and gave me a new mother. However, I did not know much but shadow memories of my earliest childhood until I was thirty. When I was eleven, my parents told me I had had another mother who had died, but not how. When I was thirty and having some health problems, I was encouraged by my doctor to find out more. My dad had died by then, and so Mom was left to give me the details.

I wish I could've talked about my biological mother's death with my father, but I think my parents did the best they could for the times we were living in, and that is all anyone can do. I though have had to reconcile these stories of my being, these mothers, within myself. That reconciliation leads me back to those symbols of life's comforts and inspiration, and eventually I hope will help towards an inner reconciliation of the life I shared with my husband to the life I live now.

Knowing the way we became a family—Mom, Dad, and me—and that there was another mother—led me on something of a treasure hunt as a child, for clues to this other mother. Still, I have only a few things that were hers, things that give me a little glimpse into this woman who loved me. I have an old recipe box with white cards that actually have her writing, a couple of letters that she wrote to my father, her wedding dress, a few pictures, a couple of books. I know that she, as I do, liked the writings of Thomas Merton.

Yet I think the most precious thing I have is her set of silver flatware, not because of the value of silver or that it does gleam on the Christmas dinner table, but because it is from both the mother that gave birth to me and the mother that raised me. That box of silver forks, knives, and spoons is a small miracle of reconciling parts of my life. The set was once incomplete, needing forks to make up the right number of place settings. When I was in college, Mom decided she would complete that set for me. Now, I have to admit that when she gave me forks for my nineteenth birthday, I was anything but thrilled.

"What did you get for your birthday?" my college roommate asked.

"Forks," I answered. Even more depressing at the time was that I thought all of my friends had forgotten my birthday. What I didn't know was that they had planned a surprise party on the roof of the dorm. I still remember the delight in that party—these girls had gone to all of this trouble for me!

And now, many years later, those forks have become a symbol of these two mothers loving me together. The wooden silver chest is marked with the imprint of an architect's triangle that my father rested on it through its many years in storage, before Mom completed the set. I wouldn't refinish that chest for the world, for that includes Dad too in this more female, silverware symbol. Through Dad, I can even include my third mother—his mother, Annie, who was the grandmother who raised me until I was four and continued to be a part of my life until she died. It was a sadness to me as a child that Mom and my grandmother could not find a peace as friends. Now, I see that my grandmother felt a child was being taken from her as my father remarried, and that Mom was in a tough role of becoming a mother with a grandmother who wouldn't support her in that role. Then, I just couldn't understand why they didn't love each other as I loved them both. It is easy to keep my biological mother's mother, a grandmother I never knew, in this memory box, for I have found a way to connect with her through learning to cook the traditional Greek dishes I know she would have cooked. I have taught my girls how to make moussaka and baklava as well. We often serve these over holidays.

The last woman in my life in a grandmother role was Mom's mother, Leena Smith. In the silver chest are even some decorative serving spoons she gave to me, though she truly never accepted me as a grandchild, something again I just didn't understand as a child. I called her "Mrs. Smith," until I was old enough to suggest myself that maybe I could call her by her first name. I knew better than to suggest I call her Meme as my cousin did. I knew his school picture would always sit in a heavy silver frame, front and center, on the living room organ while a small one of me might be found in a back room somewhere. And yet I keep Leena's spoons there, with the memories of my parents and grandmothers, because they are decorated with impressions of fruit and vines. I remember one day when I was a girl and Mom had no where else to leave me than with her mother for an afternoon; Mrs. Smith and I found a common moment in our lives when she taught me how to make arrangements from dried flowers and fruits.

Midsummer, 2010
Survival Snapshot: Listening

"There are always gifts in the worst of life's difficulties," I tell a troubled friend on the phone. These are not just consoling words; I believe this is true—even in the worst of circumstances. I add, "I don't remember signing up on the gift registry for being the survivor of a mother who committed suicide or a husband who became someone I no longer recognized." I am reminded of another mom who once told me that the summer Bible School song she was teaching included a verse about Jesus healing Peter's mother-in-law—a gift that Saint Peter had not asked for (and perhaps not really wanted)!

Looking for gifts in the tragedies of our lives is one of the gifts my sister of the heart, Marie, taught me as she lived to the fullest even as she was dying. We visited the bookstore after chemotherapy sessions. She carried her reverse feeding tube—so that solid food didn't get clogged in her intestines (her milky nutrients were really sustaining her and were injected into the port) in one of her homemade quilted bags that she took out with her so that we could stop at a restaurant and she could eat some real food. At home, we watched movies and talked and sat in the garden. We talked with all of our kids and still shared birthdays. And we cried together over her illness, over my divorce. She said that cancer had given her a gift of spending time with me, with her family, with her beloved garden, dogs, and cats—with watching the hummingbirds.

Did she wish for many more springs of seeing the hummingbirds return? Did she want to see her son graduate from high school, her oldest daughter's wedding, for more of life's adventures? Of course she did. But she lived the most she could through the most difficult of times. And I carry her with me now in life's best—and worst—times.

One time when I was going to visit my mother, when she still lived in another city, I somehow took the wrong turn even though I had driven that road many times. This was soon after my separation from my husband, soon after my friend's death, and now I think it is a wonder I could drive at all! During this time, I remember running over curbs and starting the wrong way down one-way streets. I had learned to turn around and keep going. But this time, as I got farther and farther down a long country road, I kept seeing signs for an antique store. What I didn't realize was that the signs started a good ten miles before the store. But rather than turning around, it became a quest to reach this store, which was in a tiny community called Nonesuch—named, I later learned, because someone said there was none such place.

Yet there was such a place. What I remember most about this trip was that I could feel Marie there with me as I drove and drove. It was like we were on one of our adventures together again—just seeing what was out there.

Do I wish she could be with me, actually sitting in the car again? Of course I do. Yet I am grateful for the gifts of her life and for the continuity of friendship beyond death.

Marie and Joseph and I were once all young together—once in college together. She, escaping from an early, abusive marriage, went through my courtship with me and I later with her when she met the husband she was married to for the rest of her life and had her children with. She called my husband "the rock," and decided to accept her new love's marriage proposal after spending a weekend with Joseph and me after we had been married for a couple of years.

This is hard to believe now, but it is true. I know Marie too saw the best in people, yet I can at least remember her opinion with some assurance that I wasn't just completely wrong about the initial stability of the man I married. Again, I am sure now that those seeds that could grow into addiction were present even then, but those were not the ones he was watering and we did not see them. Years later, as he began to change so dramatically with addiction, I asked her, "Did I just miss all of these flaws from the beginning?"

She reminded me about how she had called him "the rock." She too hoped so desperately that he would find his way through addiction darkness, back to his family. My last memory of Marie talking with Joseph is her visit for Lynn's high school graduation, that brief period of remission from the second cancer when she could still travel on her own. She was almost ready to leave when she said, "I haven't talked to Joseph. I want him to know that I can forgive him too."

I can still see her making the effort, for even then she was growing weak, to walk back up the rise to my house, going into the kitchen where Joseph sat at the table, and telling him that she wanted him to know that she too forgave him for the hurt to me and our children, people she loved. I remember her trying to make eye contact with him, but Joseph continued to just look down. Remembering this, I hurt for all of us. So many people were offering Joseph a chance, but I think now all he could hear was the condemnation from his mother and I suppose the condemnation within himself. These are what he rebelled against, never hearing the forgiveness and love.

I remember so many of my last conversations with Marie. I called every morning during the last months of her illness so we could share a few moments. Of course, we talked about how she was feeling that day and if she needed anything, but we also talked about everyday life—about the ruby-throated hummingbirds in the garden. And she came to the point of telling me, "Try, just for a while, to think about something today besides Joseph. Try to take care of yourself." I think now she was in that thin space between worlds of this earth and the life beyond. She knew more quickly than I could that he was not going to hear those words of reconciliation from either of us. She did not try to talk with Joseph again.

There is a sadness when those we have loved are not present with those we come to love later. We wish they could meet—certainly wish to get a woman friend's opinion about any man in our life!

And so there was an unexpected joy when a few months ago the man now in my life heard Marie speaking, even if only in his own mind, or perhaps in a light wind filtering through leaves in the church courtyard where Marie's ashes are interred. Clay and I were driving through the town with the church I attended with Marie so often. Having been both her matron of honor and the godmother to her three kids, Marie and I had laughed that various Episcopal priests had emphasized through these occasions my great responsibility for her and her family's well being.

Since the memorial area at the church was not yet completed when she died, we had had the funeral at the church, but her ashes had been kept and were then interred with her name engraved on a walkway brick when that courtyard garden was later finished. On the day the ashes were actually due to be interred, another friend was scheduled to have breast cancer surgery. Marie had spent an evening with this other dear friend and I knew it would be more honor to her to be at the hospital than at the interment. So, I had never actually been able to visit the spot where her ashes rested.

As we came into the town, I asked Clay if he would stop at the church. He of course agreed, and after a little winding here and there, we found the church again that I had not visited since my friend's funeral. St. Paul's Episcopal Church is, as are so many Episcopal churches, charmed with large, uneven grey stones that have stood fitted together for over a century and those red doors that once promised refuge to anyone who was a fugitive.

We walked around the church and found the small courtyard, paved with smooth bricks with the names and dates of those members who rested beside the church they had loved. I recognized some names and finally found Marie's marker along one side of the garden. Someone, I imagine one of her daughters, had placed two angels by her place. One was one of the small faceless angel figurines we both loved, this one holding a pink conch shell near her ear. I remembered my own enchantment with such shells as a child—they always seemed to whisper some wisdom that if I listened long enough I might begin to hear. I stood there several minutes, talking to Marie in my mind, and then moved over a few steps beneath one of the young trees to regain composure.

Clay moved to where I had been standing, also looking at the resting place of the friend I so wished could now talk with him—talk with me about him!

We left the courtyard and drove towards the bridge that led into Indiana. This was the same bridge I had so often taken her across to reach the larger city where she had most of her medical treatments. I also thought of crossing the bridge from Kentucky into Indiana when I was a child and my aunt would take me from Kentucky to Indiana to shop. It seemed as if we were passing into a promised land then when I was a girl!

On the bridge, Clay said to me, "When we were there by Marie's grave, I heard her speaking to me. She said, 'Everything is going to be okay.' And I felt such a sense of peace."

As with dreams and conch shells, those who have left our world of dirt and leaves and sea sometimes seem to speak in a riddle or whisper. I have wondered what she was telling him was going to be alright: the two of us, me, him, life after death—or perhaps all of these things. Perhaps like the iridescence in a hummingbird's wings and throat that causes the color we actually see to shift with the angles of light, what is revealed is what is needed for survival—for mating or protection at different times. The wings, the gorget that sometimes radiates that ruby red, don't actually change, but what is needed at that moment is what is present.

Midsummer, 2010
Survival Snapshot: "Wheel of Fortune" Court

So, finally, court day arrived. From the late winter day four months ago when I received a copy of Joseph's plea to the court to change our seven-year-old separation agreement that two years later became our divorce agreement, this legal business and legal bills have consumed way too much energy and life.

Being a reluctant learner on how addiction changes a person so completely and allows them to lie so easily, I was shocked to see Joseph's lies written in black and white. The pleas to the court claimed he had paid for a new roof on the house. Though the house could have used a new roof, there was no new roof. Suddenly my little car had become worth more than the one he had received (easily enough proved false with a quick online search). The biggest laugh was the accusation that I was storing away money while he was struggling. The money I had spent to put our children through college seemed in Joseph's mind to have been contributed by the college fairy. Somehow even my degree and profession had changed in the document. I don't know to this day if Joseph actually told his lawyer all of this, or what was in anyone's mind.

I do know that I was back again in my original divorce lawyer's office four days later; now four months later, it is court day.

In the morning, having been unable to do much but watch the third series of "Big Love" for the last few days, and read a memoir by a writing student that escaped a religious cult, and edit the first assignment from another student on Death Row (all confirmation that things really could be worse), I stumble onto the back porch with a cup of coffee. The red-tailed hawk family is especially vocal this morning, calling to each other with less of that long-distance echoing cry I hear so often, but more of a short-range call. The short call may simply be a hawk version of the, "I said breakfast is ready and we need to get going," morning call I once so often called to start the day with my own family, though there sounds to me like a note of panic in the hawks' morning conversation. I remember, too, the school mornings when I knew that if one of my kids missed the opening bell one more time, she would be in trouble and I would feel an irresponsible mother! Most likely, it is my own panic over somehow losing home and woods and hawks that I hear imposed on the hawks' morning conversation.

Mom goes with me down to the courthouse. We pass through security that since 911 and threats to a judge several years ago has now come to even our small city. I have to hold Mom's hand now when she goes up and down a curb. I did this on the way into the courthouse and each time, it startles me a little that she needs my help. And yet through these months I have needed her help with handling the legal business and bills. Again, I remember the day she said to me, "Isn't it something that you and I are the ones left to help each other now? I have thought about this a lot." Because my mom is technically my stepmother, she was perhaps referring to my father's death almost twenty-eight years ago. I suppose it is strange in some way that the man who brought us together is dead and that she is helping me stay safe from the father of my children, her grandchildren. But family is not just genes and birth, it is who is there with you in life. Death has taken both of my biological parents, addiction has changed my children's father into someone I hardly see as related now. Mom and I are holding each other up and going through security.

Upstairs, more of the adopted family, connected to me and wanting to help hold me up through this ordeal, shows up to wait outside the courtroom. The couple who have served so many years as another set of grandparents for my daughters arrive first, embracing me in a hug. I know this has been an effort as Joan has not been well. And I appreciate Harold saying that he wants Joseph to see that he, the man in the couple we once traveled and shared holidays with, is standing with me—that Joseph's behavior has not all just been okay. My Episcopal priest comes next, wearing her collar. She and her husband have a new grandchild and are leaving town in a couple of days to meet the baby, but she insisted she had time to come to court. The dear friend, Ruth, who has been with me to the mediation and all else, comes in next. Clay is standing by if I need him.

When I get home, my daughters and other friends will be checking on me. There are two cards of support from other friends in my bag. One card has two very girlie alligators on the front cover with bows and pearls. One is saying to the other, "Great purse." Inside the card, the alligator with the purse replies, "Thanks, it's my ex-husband." My friend has written, "Might as well dream big! We're all behind you all the way!" The card has kept me laughing for days.

As we all walk into the courtroom, I try to focus on all of these people who love me, not on Joseph who refuses to look at any of us, who sits with his arms folded across his chest, who looks to me now as if he hasn't smiled in years—all of the lines drawn down from his mouth. There is no one with him but his lawyer. (Joan who sees auras tells me later his is black and purple with a white flash, indicating despair and confusion and some kind of looming illness. My priest tells me the next morning that she saw no emotion at all—that he seemed to have encased himself in his own little world.) I can't feel any connection to this man I was married to for so many years. My friend, Ruth, tells me she didn't even recognize him. When she first came up to my side earlier, she had said she had seen his lawyer downstairs talking to someone she didn't know.

All I can do is try to concentrate on what is physically in front of me—the table, the yellow legal pad and black felt pen my lawyer puts in front of me. I keep fingering the blue bracelet with its angel or bird wing charm that I wore today to remind me of all of the birds that are my neighbors and inspiration—the hawks, barred owls, finches, bluebirds, hummingbirds—and angels too. We are in the midst of a Kentucky heat wave and the courtroom is at least cooler than the hot hall, but my lawyer in his suit comments on how hot it is. We all rise for the judge. She looks disheveled and hot in her robes, and I have the feeling she would rather be anywhere than in this courtroom. Or maybe it is just me that would rather be anywhere than in this courtroom.

Having all risen, we all sit down—and just when you think it can't get any crazier, it does.

Within minutes, my ex-husband's lawyer has dropped us into what I think must be the equivalent of "The Wheel of Fortune" Court of Law. The judge asks her on what basis of law she is bringing up this case after so many years.

"Any law," she says. "I'll take any law you can give me."

I think I see the judge roll her eyes. I have this bizarre image of Joseph's lawyer spinning a giant wheel and saying, "L. And I'll buy an A."

The judge asks what they hope to modify in a settlement in force over five years?

"Anything," the lawyer answers. "We'll take anything we can get." She goes on to talk about this man not having had his day in court, which makes the judge angry, as she is the one who signed off on the original divorce. The lawyer keeps using the word, "unconscionable."

I later look up "unconscionable" in a legal dictionary, to learn that it means a contract that no one in their right mind would sign and no one in their right mind would accept. In divorce agreements, there seems to be a fairly limited time frame of when you can decide you were not in your right mind. My lawyer and I later discuss that perhaps during the original of the divorce agreement, Joseph was trying to do right by me and our daughters. I wonder if, once a man has betrayed his own conscience so thoroughly and continues to do so, he can only see the rest of the world as unconscionable towards him.

The lawyers and the judge are involved now in some dance of justice and it seems that Joseph and I, the ones that "brung them to the dance" are left on our opposite corners of the room, waiting to see if anyone is going to ask us to dance. As numbers of laws are discussed, I look at the man I was married to for so long. He is still wearing the wedding ring from his recent second wife, a marriage I think my friends have taken a poll on to see how long this will possibly last. The gold ring catches a glint from the afternoon sun from one of those high windows. I feel a little stab of hurt—not as much as I would have felt even a year ago, but enough to know some hurts crawl into hiding rather than leaving completely.

As Joseph's lawyer keeps insisting that he was treated unfairly, I hear Mom starting to mumble behind me. There is little time to be lost in some revelry of hurt because the next thing I know she leans forward to grab my lawyer's shoulder. "George," she says, "that's not true. Why aren't you objecting?"

This brings me quickly into the present and I say, I hope soothingly, "It's okay, Mom. We've got it." I spend the next hour after all of this telling her it just wasn't a point to object—and being thankful *she* didn't actually stand up and say, "I object." Still, I look forward to being eighty-three years old when you can finally say all of the things you've wanted to say for thirty or forty years, and there is either some factor of being respected, or just ignored, that allows this.

Later, after the judge delays even hearing the case and gives Joseph's lawyer two weeks to give her a reason why she should even consider hearing going any further, when we have all left, and I am back home looking up "unconscionable," I relax a little bit. To me, unconscionable does seem a word that can be in court when there is nothing else to base anything on. I wonder again how the man who cheated on me, left me with everything from an old car broken down in the driveway and two girls to get through college to an aging dachshund that refused to eat and an aging cat that scratched the wallpaper from the shock of the family coming apart can possibly think I had been unconscionable towards him.

From my experience, I am not sure that anyone is truly in their right mind, certainly their best mind, when their marriage is coming apart. But I think Joseph was certainly more in his right mind when trying to do something right by me in at least granting me the last security of our home than he is now when guilt has gone underground or been soothed by a myriad of women.

Two days before this hearing, a friend who had volunteered where my husband had worked when we were married, finally told me that she had seen him—while we were still married and living together—leaving often with a female co-worker. I have no final proof of an affair at this point, but another puzzle fit into place when my friend told me what she had seen. In a moment, I was back to hearing him talk about, "Poor Mollie, who was going through a second divorce." The change from begging me to keep trying and go back to marriage counseling to some switch into, "I want to see who is out there," falls into place. The work dinner where he didn't see any need to take me along had a whole new meaning. Running into this woman after the divorce and having her show me a diamond from yet another man she had married by then, and when I said, "Well, tell Joseph hello," her studied look and "Oh, we don't need to do that," made sense. Or was it one of the other co-workers? Names rush through my mind.

The knowledge that while I was trying to do all of those exercises to get our marriage back on the road while he was already on yet another infidelity highway, hurt that day when I found it out years later, and I wondered why I would be given such knowledge now, why this late revelation would be any part of God's timing.

But after court I realized it was to help me buck up within about any false guilt of somehow having been unconscionable.

With it finally settled that the lawyers can write these briefs on whether to hear or not to hear any of this, my lawyer says we can leave. Nothing is really settled, though I have—almost—decided to quit worrying about it all, about being forced to sell my home. But the pain from the glint of Joseph's second wedding ring stays with me, perhaps because Father's Day is the next week.

Midsummer, 2010
Survival Snapshot: The Last Father's Day

Father's Day, six years ago, a year after our separation, my husband and I had made a date to get new wedding rings. The day before, I had gone to a local store and picked out a pair of claddagh rings. I love that Irish symbol of the hands holding the heart with a crown above that represents love, friendship, and fidelity. I had so hoped that Joseph, too, wanted to regain those qualities in our marriage. I called him, still at his apartment, to tell him about the rings and see if he would like them. He sounded very down on the phone.

His voice reminded me of the way it had sounded over the years when he would go out of town and call home, sounding on the verge of desperation with loneliness. Then, I never quite understood this, because though I loved my family fiercely, with two small children and many responsibilities, it was a rare treat when I had a chance to be alone with a book, or a movie, or even just my thoughts. Now, I know that my husband's calls were "save-me-from-myself" calls—calls he made before what addicts call "acting out" their addiction. In counselor John Bradshaw's book, <u>Family Secrets: What You Don't Know Can Hurt You</u>, a woman described this as her addict husband calling desperately to her from a castle tower, but just as she reached the grounds, he would order the drawbridge pulled up, leaving her stranded outside.

That is how it is for the spouse and family of a sex addict. And in the years before you know there is even an addiction (for this is an easier addiction to hide than some—there is no alcohol smell on the breath; something is off but you can't ever figure out what), you find yourself standing outside of that castle, strange creatures swimming around the moat, wondering what you are supposed to do when you don't even understand what is wrong.

When Joseph would call home, sounding desperately alone, I would make   suggestions of a book or a movie, or maybe there was someone else at the conference to talk with or who would go along to dinner. I would reassure him that I loved him and put the children on the phone to say goodnight. I would hang up the phone, confused though a little touched that he missed me and the kids because I often felt we were kind of in his way at home—like furniture he was glad was there but didn't want to have to do any repairs to or polish.

When, years later, I knew of the addiction, and he was trying, or at least I think he was trying, to overcome it, when he went out of town, I gave him something that I hoped would help—a picture of the girls and me, and once a prayer card a student had sent me. For our twenty-fifth wedding anniversary, one of my gifts to Joseph was a cross with the serenity prayer that he could carry in his pocket.

When our dachshund, Wilbur, was a puppy, he ate a blood pressure pill that Joseph had dropped. We called the vet and she told us we didn't have time to get the dog to her and we had to make him throw up immediately by pouring salt down his throat. I held the dog while my husband poured salt, or maybe it was the other way around. I mainly remember thinking and saying, "He's going to die," and the children crying. We saved Wilbur, who went on to live to old age; and though he continued to love to steal anything left around, he never again ate another pill. I would sometimes hear him whining and would find him lying down next to some kind of pill, usually a dropped vitamin one my children had promised to take, his nose pointing towards the pill. I know that dog remembered that one terrible incident all of this life and was saying, "Save me from myself." And I could pick up the pill and all was well.

But I couldn't save my husband. He had to save himself.

I did try, though, even after that initial separation, to save our marriage, our intact family—to give him a space in which to try to find whatever coping skill would help him, hence the Father's Day when we had planned to get those new rings and go from there.

Six months earlier, I was driving home one night and praying for help. The girls had gone back to college, my husband was in that apartment and I knew had been meeting with women he'd met on the Internet for sex—one a younger married woman with small children. And my friend was dying.

"What," I prayed, "do You want me to do now?"

I felt a clearness of thought in that car: I needed to offer my husband forgiveness and a chance to keep our marriage together.

I know that then and now as well, family and friends thought I was not thinking straight and was only setting myself up for more hurt. And there was more hurt. But if you ask God what to do and get an answer, it is wise to follow up on that answer!

So, we went back to counseling and began a bizarre period of dating each other. I insisted he give up any of his other contacts. I guess he did—he told me and the counselor he did, but I of course have no way of knowing. He would seem to have a good time but then again would be restless, sometimes angry. In short, if I hadn't been married to this man, I wouldn't have kept dating him!

I think I knew in my heart, though I couldn't quite admit it to myself, that the husband I had known was truly lost to me when he told the counselor one night that "she is just so good and kind, always telling me she is glad I am there—and I just don't know how to respond."

Again, I had had many moments of anger myself. Certainly, I had said things to him that I never thought I would say to anyone! "Burn in Hell," comes to mind.

But in these months, I tried to come back to what is, I suppose, more my nature. Joseph had always said that one of the things he loved about me was that I was kind. What I realized though in the counselor's office was that it really didn't have much to do with my response—anger, kindness, that elusive search for unconditional love he had missed as a child. If someone could have told me what to do—how to take away the pill on the floor as I had been able to do for my dachshund, Wilbur—I would've done it. But dogs are different than people—they are willing to be saved from themselves.

As a young writer, I remember a long, frustrating period of getting notes from editors saying I had real talent (or some variation of that), but they couldn't use whatever I had sent them. The problem was they couldn't tell me anything to change—the market just didn't need this story or book. It is obviously in my nature to keep trying. In college, I struggled through second semester Calculus to pass and received a note from my professor that said, "You have passed with a D and I want you to know that I admire your persistence."

But my marriage was failing, regardless of persistence or kindness on my part. So, did I hear God wrongly? I don't think so. I asked the counselor this and she pointed out that maybe I was the only one in the relationship listening. There is a story in Jewish lore that when a man divorces the wife of his youth, even the altar cries. I think this was an opportunity for both of us to meet that ideal of a marriage overcoming all odds.

Ruth, my wise friend, said to me, "I think this was what God knew you had to do—to give the marriage every possible chance, so you could heal and move forward." That too I think is true.

But first, there was that last Father's Day. The day before, when I called about the rings and heard his low voice, I asked, "Have you changed your mind about getting new rings?"

He assured me he hadn't. Elaine was home from college and her father had said he wanted us to all go out and celebrate Father's Day. I had asked him if he wanted it to be just him and her, but he insisted he wanted us to all go out together as a family.

Knowing now what was to come, I have never understood this. I have never understood whether he simply could not make up his mind on whether to stay a part of the family, or if he wanted to make some kind of grand statement that would allow no going back. I don't know, and as one friend says about Joseph, "How could anyone know what he is going to do next? *He* doesn't know what he is going to do next!"

Whether he intended this to be an allow-no-going-back statement or not, that is what it became for me. As a mother, I would rather be sick than have a child be sick, rather be hurt myself than have my child hurt. Of all of the things my husband did, of all of the ways in which he changed into another man, the way he has treated our daughters has been the most difficult for me to understand. Before our divorce, I had said, "No one will ever love these girls as much as we do. Have you thought about how a divorce, how knowing you quit trying to overcome an addiction rather than keep your family together, will affect them?"

Joseph looked at me and said, "It won't affect them at all." I remember standing there, stunned. How was he the same man who had been so proud of those babies and held them high in his hands, pretending they were airplanes that giggled with glee, who had played "Candy Land" and read the Ramona books with those children, who had paced the family room the first night our oldest—and our youngest—took the car out alone?

Getting home from the store the night before Father's Day, I told Elaine about the rings. She, who hadn't shown much interest in Father's Day beforehand, decided to make her dad one of the sugar-free pudding pies he liked. She made the pie—butterscotch—and put DAD in chocolate chips on the top. We went to the discount store to get a card; I remember she bought a ribbon that said "Super Dad" on it.

After church the next morning, Elaine dropped me off at his apartment, the plan being that Joseph and I would go get the rings and then she would meet us for I believe a movie. (Certain scenes from that day are like mind movies, while other details are a blur.) Then, I think, we planned to have dinner and go back and have the pie.

But when I got to the apartment, instead of welcoming with a smile, Joseph just pointed towards a piece of paper on the table. I asked what it was and he just pointed again. I don't remember at that point having that cold chill that goes all the way down to the pit of my stomach when life is getting to take one of those turns when nothing will ever be the same again—when there is no turning back. I still had some remaining faith then that he would follow through on what he had said he would do.

When I picked up the paper, I saw it was a letter. For one brief second, I thought it might be a letter like the ones I had received over the twenty-seven years of our marriage, telling me how much he loved me, that he was sorry for any hurts, that he would do everything possible to make our marriage work, that he wanted us always to be together. Then, I saw the first statement: I want a permanent separation and eventually a divorce.

I remember sitting down then on the old wooden-framed couch with its tweed cushions, the couch we had bought used from my parents' neighbors and moved into our first apartment. I had been so proud of that couch and its matching end table and coffee table. The cushions were now ripped in places after its years of being our girls' playroom couch, and somehow it had found its way into an apartment Joseph shared with no one who loved him. Writing this, I wonder now where that couch ended up—it is a silly bit of sentiment I know, but I hope it found a home back with some young couple who recovered the cushions.

The words on the page began to sink into my brain. The rest is again something of a blur. I remember calling, because Joseph refused to make the call, the store that was holding the rings and telling them we wouldn't be buying rings. I remember asking him, "You know if you do this, there really will be no going back?" I don't remember any reply beyond a nod. I remember him giving me some mishmash of "notes to self" he had made before writing this letter that again mentioned I had gained weight over the years but so had everyone else, and a lot about how he didn't know what he wanted. There seemed no concern about how divorce would affect me or our children—just how it might affect Joseph himself.

I remember calling my daughter and telling her that Dad had changed his mind about us all going out and that I needed her to come and bring me the car and then he and she could go out if they wanted. "And honey," I said, "you might want to bring your Father's Day ribbon and your pie. I don't think he'll be coming back to the house."

I walked out and turned back halfway down the steps, going back to ask him for my original wedding ring that he had been keeping for me. Later, a friend laughed about this, saying, "It's at least worth something." I have debated several times since, especially when the price of gold is high, about selling that ring. But it is in those two blue boxes that contain the essence of the best years of our marriage that I have kept mainly for my children, and perhaps honestly a little bit for myself. As much as we want to wipe out history, it is part of who we are. My father, who mixed up quotes and told the wrong punch lines for jokes, sometimes reached a Zen-type wisdom in those confusions. He often misquoted poet and philosopher George Santayana's quote, "Those who do not study history are doomed to repeat it," by saying, "Those who repeat history are doomed to study it." So I keep the tokens of that history, yet put them away and release the history in these words, hoping I will neither be doomed to repeat it nor study it forever. I wore that ring constantly for twenty-six years, so it is a part not only of my history but of my children's history. My dear friend, Dora, whose parents married and divorced twice and now cannot be in the same room, wears her mother's wedding ring from her father. "Though they may not like each other," Dora has told me, "they once loved each other—and after all produced me—this is part of my life too."

I did not think through all of this then—I just wanted the ring back in case it was the only wedding ring I ever had! I put it with my silver anniversary ring. Now, those rings are for my daughters or even their children if they want them as they continue their own histories.

On what I think of as "the last Father's Day," I took back the ring and then waited on the outside steps for my girl. This part of the day is one

I remember too fully. When she pulled up in my little red car, I told her that Dad would explain the change in plans and talk as long as she wanted. I would wait in the car until she came to tell me her plans with Dad.

I can see Elaine now, with her father's height, yet with expressions and gestures that most people say are mine, going up those steps—with her carefully held pie with DAD spelled out in chocolate chips—to her father's apartment. Though there had been a long progression of events that had felt like giant cosmic scissors snipping the threads of my marriage apart, this is the snapshot that stands out in a frame of its own. Our daughter too had felt that hope for her father, for our family, when she made that pie and bought that Super Dad ribbon. I pray for a good relationship for my children with their father, and I have tried, though I am sure sometimes more successfully than others, not to make it worse; but that moment captures for me a knowledge that things would never be the same for her as well as for me with the man who had been my husband and (considering no one has yet figured out a way to suck the DNA out of a person from one parent) will always be her father.

She came back quickly, saying Dad was crying too much to tell her anything, and we went home. I took a long nap and woke up to her fixing bacon, tomato, and peanut butter sandwiches, an old Sunday supper tradition passed down from my family.

Midsummer, 2010
Survival Snapshot: Inner Ogress

Remembering that last Father's Day, it is a surprise when the brief filed by Joseph's lawyer came in a couple of weeks later, with the argument for the judge hearing his case being that he claims he never wanted a divorce and so feels he could have been coerced in signing the agreement granting me the "marital residence," as my lawyer calls it. Joseph claims now that he did this in a desperate attempt to save our marriage and from a deep sense of guilt due to my discovery of his "affinity" for Internet pornography. Joseph's affinities for massage parlor prostitutes and one-night stands with women met on the Internet are strangely enough not mentioned.

And I am amazed again—amazed that this statement has been presented just after I have written my preceding survival snapshot of that awful Father's Day, amazed that he can claim he was honestly working on our marriage. Has he really rewritten this in his own mind, or is this just another legal ploy? And I am amazed that adulteries and addictions can somehow be rewritten into an "affinity." It sounds as if I just didn't understand that he wanted to go bowling on a regular basis! I should be used by now to this whitewash job, or perhaps hogwash (a term my grandmother would've used) would be more accurate, but I never do get used to this—and perhaps that is a good thing. If I get used to this, I might be losing some of my own grounding in common sense.

I am impressed with my own lawyer's rebuttal with cases that dispute bringing such an agreement back to court—and his point that this is actually the third time it has been called into question. But I am surprisingly thrilled that he makes the point that while I have been presented as "some type of ogre," the facts show otherwise. I call my girlfriends to tell them that I am embracing my inner ogress!

Now, why should I be actually pleased that anyone thinks of me as "some type of ogre?" I guess it is because of all of those years of being a nice girl (remember my fear that this is code for wimp). Finally, at 55, I have grown teeth—even fangs—that say,

"Really, enough is enough." Not only can I defend my children, but perhaps I can finally even defend myself.

I also feel I must protect my own mother when a few days later, Mom tells me that she has seen my ex-husband at her retirement home, on a professional visit with one of the other residents. She says Joseph pretended not to see her and ran into the apartment of the lady he was visiting without even knocking, shutting the door behind him as quickly as possible.

I am truly not sure who needs protecting from whom, but the next morning I call the retirement home's director and tell her that I think my former husband is someone who could snap, and I do not want him near my mother. They promise to watch for him, to call me if he enters the building. I also call Mom and make her promise that, no matter how much she wants to confront him, she won't. I feel like I am living in a bad movie, or at least a movie about bad guys, but I have seen that cold look on his face. I know the Mr. Hyde that can emerge from underneath all of the whitewash.

It is though not easy for me to walk with the ogress within. In her book, Goddesses in Older Women: Archetypes in Women Over Fifty, Jean Shinoda Bolen talks about how, within us, the archetypes (I would clarify the forces that shape us from story, myth, and even religion) can at points in our lives be: "the goddesses of transformative wrath. They come to the fore when it is time to take action to charge an unacceptable situation, when *enough is enough*....The most prominent goddesses of transformative wrath are depicted as nonhuman in appearance. The Egyptian goddess Sekhmet has the head of a lion and the body of a woman."

Clay, who encourages toughness in me, found me this book at one of the used library sales we love to visit. I imagine he just saw the mythology reference and knowing how much I draw on mythology in my writing, pulled it out for me. But as often happens, someone who loves us gives us what we need right when we need it. I read this book as I got ready to face the initial court encounter and tried to imagine myself walking with Sekhmet, that lion-headed goddess who was both a goddess of wrath and of healing. Perhaps I succeeded a bit and that is why I can actually be conceived by at least my ex-husband and his lawyer as an ogress. I am thinking an ogress could possibly look something like Sekhmet.

However, writing this, I am drinking out of a coffee cup that has Sylvester the Cat printed on it—one of my favorites as it reminds me of my Charlotte tomcat. Like most cats, I would rather contemplate life in the sun and have a playful game with the resident dog than fiercely confront anyone. Though Charlotte was a good mouser, I am not even too keen on throwing a half-living mouse up in the air and playing toss with it. A bowl of chocolate chip ice cream will be fine. But it is good to know that when backed into a corner, I have teeth and claws.

Late Summer, 2010
Survival Snapshot: Meatloaf

I saw my doctor yesterday, who lately wants to see me more often because he is concerned about what stress is doing to me—so far, as in every life crisis with my husband, now ex-husband, I have managed to gain ten pounds. My doctor assured me again that I am coping well, am quite coherent; he thought it was funny that meatloaf was what I gravitate towards in stress, not even so much for comfort, but because they make it at the local Piggly Wiggly and all I have to do is heat it and pretend I am still cooking. He thought I should write a book where the character eats meatloaf whenever she is stressed, told me to check my blood pressure at home, and to reassure my mother that the weight would go back down as I got through this and that I was in all great likelihood going to outlive her.

Mom told me yesterday morning that the son of a friend of hers had died. Actually, Mom's grieving friend was the lady who had sold us that wooden couch set I had loved so much as a newlywed. The son was my high school classmate and had died from congestive heart failure. He too was an only child and his mother a widow—and he too was carrying too much weight. "Now," Mom had asked, "who is going to take care of his mother? If something happens to you, who is going to take care of me?"

As I updated my doctor about the current legal proceedings, he stepped back, his eyes widening and his mouth forming that O of disbelief when I told him about the ogre imagery. He has been my doctor for years and has seen me through this ordeal of the last seven years, commenting often that I have an abundance of nurturing qualities, but need to take care of myself. Not especially wanting an order for a speedy follow-up appointment, I do not tell him about my recent wonderings about ogres and angels.

Angel means messenger, and I wonder if God doesn't use ordinary people as messengers at times, even ordinary people that are a bit ogre-ish. If I wrote in a novel about the two encounters I have had where I wonder if I have met angels, one in a somewhat ogre-ish form, I am guessing they would be seen as unbelievable in the course of the novel—that I would lose what Coleridge called "the willing suspension of disbelief." So, never finding a place to put these true stories into fiction, I believe they belong in Survival Snapshots.

The first angelic visitation occurred before Joseph's admission of relapse into pornography addiction (and as I later learned, into live sexual encounters as well). My family was on our way to visit the college that Elaine eventually attended. From home to college was an eleven-hour drive, much of it through the endless cornfields of Illinois. Somewhere in Illinois or Wisconsin, we stopped to eat at a Denny's Restaurant. Four family members riding in a car for hours, three of them (the daughter looking at the college and the two parents) nervous and one of them bored (the daughter not looking at the college, who wasn't really convinced all of this looking with her sister would prepare her for her later college visitations) are unlikely to have been the picture of the ideal family. But as we sat in that Denny's, eating, I noticed an older couple at the table next to us. The man—just an ordinary fellow—kept studying my family. I smiled at him and he nodded.

After a bit, the man and his wife got up to leave, but halfway to the cash register, he turned back and came over to our table. He spoke directly to my husband and said, "I want you to realize that you have a beautiful family. Treasure them." My husband said nothing, so I thanked the man. Again, he nodded at me, but his focus was clearly towards my husband. "Sometimes," he said, "these things need to be said."

Later that night in the too-crowded motel room, I fussed about how far this would be from home, and Elaine got angry with me. Being the mature mother, I cried and spent an eternity in the tiny motel bathroom. When I finally came out of the bathroom, we laughed about what that man would say about our family if he could see us at the end of the day. But, now, I think he would've told my husband the same thing. We were his beautiful family, and family is to be treasured. I only wish my husband had been able to hear the message.

Late Summer, 2010
Survival Snapshot: Ogres and Angels

The second stranger-than-fiction, angelic moment happened after the meeting with the ordinary fellow at Denny's. Joseph and I were divorced. I was beginning to adjust to being divorced, to having the freedom from wondering when the next bombshell would drop (this time being before Joseph tried to take away my home). I'd begun finally to trust enough to spend time with Clay. But I still didn't feel I did divorce very well. Maybe no one does, but I was sure that some angel-in-charge had misread the script for my life. I had discovered that divorcing a man doesn't always mean you quit loving him—quit liking him, yes; and I had found out how closely love and hate truly are connected. For me, then and even now, there is this odd combination of loving the man I married and raised my children with, and hating the man who destroyed that life we had built together— and yet this is the same man. Those two personalities—the real person and the one absorbed by addiction and all of its consequences actually exist in the same body, so that the person you love and you hate really are one. I have said to my girls, "If your dad could come back to himself, I think he would be appalled at what he is doing."

Any fresh news still felt like opening that old wound. I asked Joseph right before the divorce if he didn't miss home—miss me? He told me he didn't. That I couldn't understand—even if he was having a jolly time, didn't he miss at least what we had had together? Didn't he miss being an intact family when the girls visited home? I couldn't understand what had replaced home and family for him. When I stopped by to get papers signed one Sunday, it looked as if he was dying his hair and there was a dead rose on the table. It didn't quite look like the swinging bachelor life to me. One daughter had referred to Joseph's first apartment as "the bachelor pad from Hell." This one was, I guessed from the girls' description of the first place, a little better, but again, didn't he miss home?

All I knew from my kids was that he had seen some woman a while back who owned a bed and breakfast in a forested area across the river in the next state.

One innocent day, Clay called to ask if I would go along with a woman he had talked to at a Native American gathering that had a friend visiting from Norway and wanted to see the archeological site where we volunteer. I said, "Sure." Later, he confessed that he had just had a feeling I needed to meet this woman.

Clay and I drove across the state border to pick up the woman, Rosie, and her Norwegian guest, Thor.

We met them at a park across the river. Clay just introduced me by my first name and Rosie introduced Thor. Thor got in the front seat with Clay and Rosie got in the back seat with me. They were both middle-aged. Rosie had long, dark hair and was about my could-lose-thirty-pounds size. Thor—well, Thor did remind me just a little of a Norwegian ogre. He was short and balding and had a mumbly, grumbly kind of voice that was hard to understand, but he seemed a nice enough fellow.

In the front seat, Clay began pointing out landmarks to Thor. In the back seat, I was discovering that Rosie had few inhibitions about talking about her personal life. "I'm looking for my third husband," she told me. She told me she had been widowed once and divorced from the second husband. What about me? I said I was divorced. "I've met a lot of losers on the Internet," she said. "How about you?"

"Uh," I said, "I'm just with him." I pointed towards Clay in the front seat, who I thought seemed to have one ear pointed towards the back! I decided to try to shift the conversation away from dating. "So, what do you do?" I asked.

"I run a bed and breakfast," she answered. A little ding when off in my mind, but I ignored the bell. There were lots of people who ran bed and breakfasts.

By this time, we were getting further into Kentucky. I asked where the bed and breakfast was located.

She told me, in the forest. Ding, ding. But, I thought, "What are the chances?" I mean, what are the chances that I would be riding in a car next to a woman my ex-husband had seen in the back seat, and a man in the front seat named Thor next to my present man?

We chugged a little further down the road and she asked me what my ex-husband did. I told her. She turned and looked at me with wide eyes. I felt queasy. "What's his name?" she asked. I whispered his name. "I went out with him!" she said. Ding, ding, ding.

At this sterling moment, we pulled into a restaurant for lunch. I somehow managed to find a way out of the car, pulling Clay aside as we walked towards the restaurant door and whispering, "She went out with my ex-husband." We went inside the restaurant and I made a bolt for the ladies' room.

In the stall in the ladies' room, I found myself unable to get the nerve to leave the stall. Desperately, I called Ruth on my cell phone. "You won't believe this," I began. Ten minutes later she, had gasped with me long enough that I thought I could walk out of the stall and join Clay, Rosie, and Thor in the restaurant.

Clay introduced Thor to the wonders of Kentucky catfish while I ate something—I have no idea what—in stunned silence. Clay told me later that Rosie had wondered aloud if she should go check on me in the ladies' room. "We girls have to stick together," she had said. He had persuaded her not to follow me. Rosie whispered to me, "I hope I didn't upset you."

"Oh, no," I lied. "What are the chances?"

The rest of the afternoon went something like this:

Rosie: "I never dated a divorced man who said so many good things about his ex-wife. He told me you were brilliant."

Me: "Huh?"

Rosie: "He said he'd been happily married for almost thirty years and just didn't know what had happened."

Me: "Well, that I can tell you...."

Rosie: "Wow! He told me he never looked at porn—that he thought men who did were infantile." Pause. Gasp. "I hope I didn't see him while you were still married. I thought you had left him for another man."

Me: "Huh? Uh, uh. Huh?"

She told me that Joseph had cried over the girls, said he missed home so badly, and that it seemed the divorce had broken his heart. I said, "Huh?" This was all so opposite of what he had told me.

Somehow, we got through a tour of the archeological site, though each time Clay would talk to Thor for any length of time, Rosie would begin to tell me, "Oh, and another thing…." Finally, I told her that I just really didn't think I could talk about this anymore.

We piled back into the car—men in front again, women cozily in back—and started heading back towards where we had left Rosie's car—an hour away. All I could think of was to go home and call every girlfriend I knew to see what they made of this mysterious encounter. Clay chose to stop at every interpretive sign, railroad track, and rock along the way to tell our guests any possible local lore. Now, these stories are normally one of the things I love about traveling with him, but during this time, I thought 100 times about jumping out of that car and thumbing a ride back home. Rosie told me about how Joseph had told her he and his wife had had a wonderful sex life.

Finally, we got them back to the park. Rosie gave me her phone number, which I have never called, though Clay received a mailer sometime later about the bed and breakfast with her listed with a new last name. I guess she found that third husband!

I puzzled over this encounter all night and called my ever-patient priest, Liz, in the morning about coming in and talking.

She listened with her patient reserved manner, though I am sure her mouth did fall open at least once. "Don't tell me…."

So, why did she think I had met these people?

She asked me what I thought.

I said that perhaps this was the only way I could learn that Joseph really had valued our marriage, our family, and at least had some regrets. It was also obvious he wasn't going to tell the truth to another woman. At the same time, this all confirmed that he was lost in lies—lost to me—and yet my confidence in what we had once had, in my own part of the marriage and me myself (brilliant, sexy, or not) recovered at least a little.

Liz nodded and suggested that perhaps Thor had been an angel.

Clay later laughed—a lot—over the angel suggestion. But I am not so sure there wasn't a bit of angel that day in our Norwegian visitor that drew us all together on the back roads of Kentucky. Perhaps there are times when we can all be messengers for God, and times when we can receive messages from the most unlikely angels—even those that we might've cast as ogres.

Reflecting on my back roads day with Rosie, Thor, and Clay, I have been contemplating how Clay became an unexpected gift in my life.

"I don't know if this is biblically based in any way," my mother says, as she often begins some passing-on of wisdom, "but I think God sometimes sends the right person into your life at the right time. And I think God sent Clay into your life when you needed him."

The Monday after what I think of as "the last Father's Day," I was on the phone with a friend and had just told her about that horrible day and that I knew at last that my marriage was dead. "I am just waiting now," I told her, "to see what door God opens next."

The phone's call-waiting buzz came at that very moment. Always thinking an incoming call could be one of my daughters or my mom, I asked my friend to hold while I answered the other call.

I knew that southern voice, reminding me of Kentucky soil—deep and just a bit gravelly—on the other end of the phone. It was a colleague I had volunteered with for a number of years at an archeological site where I give school tours for children about the prehistoric Native American people that once called that land home. I discovered this place years ago when Lynn was so interested in archeology. We volunteered together and when she grew up and went on to other ventures, I kept volunteering. I am fascinated with these ancient people that left no written record, but left a world of artifacts—pots with human, duck, possum, and bear faces and mythological creatures with a bear's face and a turtle's shell or a man's face and the wings of a bird. I love to tell their story.

I had always enjoyed talking with Clay. It seemed he could do everything: make pottery the way the ancients had, make cordage out of dogbane plants, knap arrowheads. We talked about the land and people, and about our own lives a bit—my children, his granddaughter. I was always impressed with his kindness towards the children, the visitors, and me. Once he had made a pottery replica of a medicine pipe that interested me. As I handed it back, he said, "Just put that in your pocket and keep it."

He always had a smile for me and some interesting bit of lore to share, but I knew little more about him than that he had a granddaughter that he met at the school bus and bought Little Debbie cupcakes and cookies for as her after-school snack. I had seen him at a couple of other Native American events during the long period of ups and downs after my formal separation, and had told him briefly about my husband's erratic behavior.

I hope I only talked to Clay briefly about the pain and confusion I was experiencing, but during betrayal, separation, and divorce, my mouth seemed to have become a leaky faucet that I couldn't totally shut off when anyone—and I do mean anyone—asked, "How are you today?" He told me later that he could tell from my whole expression and manner that something had gone dreadfully wrong for me—that a vivaciousness in me had disappeared.

But I was trying to keep my part of life as normal as possible. I kept teaching writing, though there were days when I wondered if anything I critiqued truly made sense. It seemed a good sign that no students requested another instructor, citing instructor insanity as the reason for transfer. I kept doing things with my children when they were home and sent care packages of cookies and chocolates, of cute sticky tab notes and holiday decorations to them at college. I made myself go to church, usually early where I would sit and drink coffee with fellow parishioners. I went out weekly with a group of girlfriends that we jokingly called our coven. I kept attending programs on subjects of interest that I still hoped to write about once I could write anything again but the poetry of heartbreak. I attended library programs.

At a program at the library on a local archeological site, I talked briefly to Clay—mercifully only about that archeological site. He told me he knew how to get there if I wanted to go sometime. I knew that he often was willing to take people out to see archeological and historical sites in the area, so I jotted down my phone number and said I would—to give me a call sometime when he planned to go.

After the last Father's Day, that brief conversation with Clay, months earlier, was certainly the last thing on my mind that Monday morning. And this again I think was God's timing, for otherwise, I guess I would've just called girlfriend after girlfriend that day and eaten a bag of chocolates. So, when he asked if I wanted to trek out to the archeological site, I said I did, adding (mouth faucet threatening to flood anything I said) that my husband had finally decided to call it completely quits on our marriage, so getting out would do me good. All he said was that he had thought my husband could go too if he had wanted. I laughed and said that no, it was just me, and arranged to meet him at a store near the road to the site. I knew that Elaine would sleep a long part of the morning and so left her and Wilbur the dachshund curled in bed and thought: "So, girl, off on an adventure."

When I was a child, my dad and I called little trips to the library or the ice cream store, or even to his architecture office housed in an old train station where he would take me on Saturdays to sort through barrels of mail or play with the Matchbox cars he put around his model buildings, great adventures.

Adventures are what Clay and I call our times together. On our first adventure, as we looked at the leftover ground that had once housed an ancient village of people that too would have had joys and heartbreak, I poured out my own heart to Clay. He is a kind man, though I doubt he would admit this, and somehow saw me in this woman who hardly recognized herself anymore. Our friendship began.

The friendship and the adventures are still continuing and over these years our friendship has developed into a romantic friendship. And I am grateful for this man who smiles at me as though I am the one he has been waiting for to walk into the room, who makes me laugh, who can share with me things he has not told anyone else, with whom I can be myself without trying to meet some agenda no one ever gave me. I am grateful that he has been here to help me with emergencies with my girls, with moving my mom, with burying my old pets, and yet understands when the girls are home that they are my priority. "Every farmer knows," he tells me, "not to separate the cow from the calf." Yet he has often volunteered to take me and the girls—and their assorted friends—out for dinner. I can turn to him for consultation or solace.

I am even grateful that he would let me help him through a hospital stay when he had a knee replaced and suffered a series of complications—

that I could sit with him through an evening of terrible pain and calm him as I might anyone I love until he could sleep. And I am grateful that he is grateful for what I am able to give, that when the hospital asked if I were family and I started to go into my stumbling explanation of I was not his wife, but I was the one there, he just said, "Yes." He began to explain that in some tribes there was a word for someone closer than a friend, but his son said, "Dad, just put her name on the paper"—and he did.

One morning about a year ago, Clay said he had something for me. "First, you have to say yes," he said.

Always one to love surprise presents, I said, "Yes," but then seeing a black box, I said, "Well, I mean maybe. Oh, what is it?"

In the box was, to my relief, not a ring but a claddagh necklace, the small symbol of the hands clasped around the heart with the crown of loyalty and the words: Friendship, Loyalty, Love, engraved beneath. Clay wanted to share those hopes with me, and so I was saying yes to that adventure of friendship, loyalty, and even love—though I am content to travel that road with Clay without having a definite destination.

This morning, I woke up, wanting somehow to include this vital snapshot in this book, yet unsure I could find the words to describe this heart union that has been given to me later in life, when I was more ready to join a convent than to care again for one certain man. I reached into the box where I keep the claddagh necklace only to find the box empty. A brief second of panic was followed by the memory that last night I had put the claddagh necklace in the small, cloth pouch I keep beside that box. In the pouch I keep a heart locket that my daughters gave me with a picture of the two of them in the locket. The silver chain of the locket and the gold chain of the claddagh had tangled together in the night.

At times, it feels that the strands of my life do tangle together—there are moments when the worlds collide and it is hard for me to find my balance in a tangle of emotions. I go somewhere with Clay that I once went with my husband and I have to reclaim it anew in this present time, enriching a good memory with another or repairing a painful memory with new metal. My children and I share memories of a time when their father and I and they were a whole family—memories still treasured, even though I have put the pictures away. We have spent the last several Christmas Eves with Clay, Mom, and other people who care. We share Elaine and Lynn's newest Christmas stories from their own elves that I have written for them since they were babies. I still put up the stockings one of their godmothers gave me when they were little, but I decorate the tree now with the storyshuck dolls (cornshuck dolls with their own stories) that I make, give, and sell, instead of the collection of family decorations we added to for so many years. I have put away those ornaments of "Our First Christmas," and "New Home," and "Baby's First Christmas." I have wrapped and stored the scribbled hearts cut with a child's hand that Elaine and Lynn gave Mom and Dad before the children even thought of buying presents. To see such hearts now makes me focus too much on those earlier Christmases and on the ones I expected to have when my girls were grown. As they form their own homes, I will pass on to my daughters these ornaments when they have room to keep them. I could not throw away those childhood gifts our children gave to both of their parents any more than I could actually throw away my own heart. Yet it is difficult to read my own heart, especially the heart tissues that love my children's father but are so damaged that I can no longer sort out the healthy tissues of that love from the dead tissue.

Heart problems—the kind you can go to the doctor for and take nitroglycerin tablets to relieve—run in my family. My father went to have a cardiac study done at the Cleveland Clinic when I was six years old. Twenty years later when he wrote them about the possibility of a bypass operation, he showed me the reply. The reply essentially said, couched in medical terms, that the clinic was surprised he was still alive. The extent of artery blockages throughout the body would not have predicted a survival until his only daughter was grown and having a child of her own. The vessels around the aorta had enlarged, forming an anastomosis, an alternate pathway for the flow of blood to the heart.

I think that along with the physical miracle of the heart, our spiritual, and emotional heart, that symbol of what we hold dearest to us, is also capable of being nourished by new pathways. There is no doubt damage done to those valves of the heart by betrayal and the failure of love to mend those arteries we once were sure would last a lifetime, but there are other roads that can unexpectedly enlarge in our lives, that can bypass the pain so that we can take tentative breaths again and feel our heart continue to beat.

Almost Autumn, 2010
Survival Snapshot: Nest Box

The seasons and I have moved into the first day of September, the 100 degree days of this oppressive summer finally beginning to relax into cooler mornings and evenings. The ruby-throated hummingbirds are even more territorial than usual around the nectar I put out as they stoke up with fat to make their long migration from Kentucky to Central America. They will almost double their weight for their long journey. Some will not survive, but now I know from a hummingbird seminar I recently attended that those who will wing so rapidly in front of the kitchen window next April and May before I have put out the nectar feeder are likely the ones returning to their summer home, to my home. I bought more native trumpet creeper at the seminar, which I have faithfully watered since in its black plastic pot on the back porch, so that I can plant it in the next few weeks to welcome the hummers back again next year.

I only occasionally hear the red-tailed hawks now, their high cries replaced by the alternately soothing caws and frantic communication of crows. One day I find the gift of an iridescent blue-black crow feather dropped near the house. My thoughts have begun to turn again to my novel, <u>Learning the Language of Birds</u>, which I was writing when I opened the mailbox that February day to find a copy of the legal motion from my former husband's lawyer pleading with the court to change our divorce agreement, to force me to sell my home—to disrupt my life all over again.

Last week, my lawyer sent me a copy of the judge's decision refusing to reopen the agreement, stating that Joseph had no grounds for all of his claims of unfairness. It takes a few days for the relief to penetrate through the anxiety of the last months, but one night in the middle of dreams I wake up to feel my muscles unknotting, my body relaxing into the mattress. I begin sitting on the back porch again in the cooler evenings, listening to the last resurrection chorus of this year's cicadas.

I am afraid to relax too much for fear that Joseph will do something else to invade the tenuous peace and new life I have found again since his betrayal and our separation and divorce, and now having overcome this latest legal battle. Having run out of legal options, now what? Throughout these entire months, I think Joseph has called both me and later my mom and hung up, leaving only one message of a song playing over and over, "What do you want of me?" Since the number is blocked and I don't have money or time to spend on having calls traced, I have no absolute proof. Strange calls have been a pattern since our divorce—blocked calls to me all day on his birthday, hang-up calls on our anniversaries of marriage and divorce. My lawyer tells me that Joseph is a miserable man, that his present home life appears to be very unstable. I do not know whether my lawyer hopes this will make me feel better myself, or if he might be warning me to be careful of Joseph, or my own heart.

Gail, my best friend from high school, cautions me not to let Joseph have any power over my thoughts—not to worry, or as my mom says, "Don't borrow trouble."

I usually respond that I don't borrow trouble; it just keeps finding me and that I have needed to stay prepared. But I understand what they are saying: remember the Bible verse about not a sparrow falling to the ground without God knowing.

Of course, the concern is that I don't want to fall to the ground, God knowing or not—I want to keep flying and roosting and living!

This summer, I kept Elaine's eighty-five pound greyhound, Emmett, while she was teaching at a summer camp. He was quite a change from my lifetime of dachshunds (and one cat), but we found a routine that worked. I learned to wind his leash around my wrist so that if he took off into a sprint, it might break my wrist, but I wouldn't lose my grand-dog. I figured out, more or less, how to get up two flights of steps with an eighty-pound dog, thrilled to see me after a trip to the grocery, winding himself back and forth around my feet as he ran up and down the stairs. No picking this dog up in my arms! We found an evening routine of walk, poop, eat, and then Emmett would lie on his back by the stone fireplace, all four of those long legs waving in the air. I would sit on the sofa where I could see him and remember that a dog is the heart of the home.

Recently, Clay came up my back steps with a stone dachshund and sat it on the back porch. "To remind you," he said, "that Wilbur's spirit is still with you." He asked if I wanted to put it on the grave.

"Keep Wilbur's spirit stone on the porch," I said, "to welcome a new dog when I am ready."

When Elaine came home, Emmett ran between the two of us, but finally settled back into following her instead of me, though I still was graced by a greeting and a lick. One day when Elaine saw me putting ice into a glass, she commented that I never used to use ice in my water. It is odd that such a little fact pointed out change to her. Before she was born, I had kept ice cube trays in the freezer, but when I was writing and raising my girls, I think ice cube trays were one of those many little things I just cut out in order to both find the spare minutes both to read books with my children and to write books myself. "Everything changes," Elaine said. I think I said something about change being a part of life and growing—one of those "wise mother" statements that insist on flowing out whenever I talk to my grown kids. But now, I think that yes, many things change. Some of the hummingbirds will not make it across the gulf and some will lose their way, blown by winds no one knew were coming their way, and yet, like those hummingbirds that will overwinter safely and return, life has a returning rhythm that is comforting, along with the necessity and joy of growth.

When Elaine and Lynn were babies, I sang them each their own lullaby: "All the Pretty Horses" for Elaine and "All through the Night" for Lynn. Sometimes, tired or distracted, or just wanting to add something that pertained to the day, I would change a word in the lullaby. The barred owls that sing me to sleep so many nights with their "Who, who, who cooks for you?" will again raise their young next spring. The young seem to have a difficult time getting down the call and sometimes for several nights I hear, "Who, who—who—wh—hoooo." But eventually the parent owls teach the young the song. Just as the basic comforting rhythm of my lullabies comforted my babies to sleep, and I hope will be a comfort to them throughout life, the owls will keep passing down their songs for generations.

We all try to find a safe home, both a physical place and a place within ourselves where we can sing our songs. We need a place where we and those we love can return to the fidelity of what is true for us and make changes as needed, adjusting the rhythm to keep singing—to keep a continuity for our nestlings so that they too can learn to fly.

Autumn is the time to open and clean out the bluebird nest box that sits just the right height in my backyard for eastern bluebirds. The nest box is a busy place from January, when the bluebirds begin to check out the nest sight, to when the bluebirds fledge and the wrens build another next on top and raise their young, usually followed by another nest by the bluebirds. Last fall I couldn't pry open the box with its high rise apartments of nests jamming the door and left it through the winter. When the bluebirds began to check out the box in the new year, I fretted until I watched a pair of bluebirds flying in and removing the twigs one by one and then the bits of grass that filled the box. Within a few days, they were ready to build a fresh nest in that old faithful nest box.

This summer the bluebirds left one bright blue feather sticking out of the last nest, but now it is fading almost to the gray of the aging wood of the box. The birds, or I, will clear the box clean so that the bluebirds can rebuild their nest again next year.

Approaching Autumn Again, 2011
Survival Snapshot: Limping and Soaring

I want to add another snapshot to this picture album—one just taken as we approach another autumn. It is the last day of August, 2011. This Labor Day weekend, Clay and I will participate in an old-fashioned harvest fair. He will make Native American pottery and I will tell stories. My father died twenty-nine years ago on Labor Day weekend, so he is strongly on my mind as I prepare the stories. I still miss him, but I feel him with me as I share my stories—all of my stories!

Last weekend, I attended a bridal tea for a church friend's daughter. Then Clay was meeting me at the church. On the way to the church, I stopped to pick up a prescription at the local pharmacy. A woman wearing sunglasses came up next to me. As she asked about her medicine, there was something familiar about her calming voice. I was still trying to place that voice when she turned to me and said, "Annie—it's me." When she took off her glasses, I realized it was Penny, our last marriage counselor, who had worked so hard to help our marriage. Ultimately when I told her Joseph refused help, she had assured me that I and the girls really would be okay. "But Joseph," she had said, "I don't know."

Now, approximately seven years later, she was asking me, "How are you?" She gave me a big hug.

"Fine," I answered, immediately wishing I had sounded more enthusiastic.

She tells me that she (widowed soon after our counseling sessions ended) has remarried and introduces me to her husband.

I feel that I should have some kind of like response, but I laugh and say, "I haven't." She laughs too, but looks at me a bit more intently. She was our most caring counselor. I tell her that Joseph did try to take me to court again, so is taking no responsibilities unless forced. She is nodding now, closer still to counselor mode. I assure her that the judge didn't ultimately hear his case and that though it cost me thousands in legal fees to get there, I am—again—fine. I say, "I do have a friend." She looks a little bit relieved at that and I want to say I'd be fine regardless, but really, she does just want me to be well. I suppose being able to open my heart to another is a sign of wellness. I tell her briefly about my girls off on new adventures and we hurry off to the rest of our days. It feels to me as if I am limping as I leave the store.

In the car, I breathe a minute and then start towards the church. At the tea, the mother of the bride passes around long slips of paper so that we can all write down advice. I sigh, wishing she had asked for recipes instead. I settle on: "It is natural for women to take care of everyone, but remember to take care of yourself too. Treat yourself as you would your best friend." Marie's spirit feels very close.

After the tea, when I meet up with Clay, I tell him that it is one of my limping days. He told me once when speaking of his own long-ago divorce, that you have to keep walking, but some days you do walk with a limp.

We browse around the art galleries and shops and then have dinner at a new restaurant. The catfish is the best I have ever had. He takes me back to my car, still parked at the church, and thanks me for being me. On this limping day, it is the best thing he could have said.

I feel tired driving home and am glad to come home to my woods. I sit on the back porch, listening to the cicadas, now in their full buzzing hum, and watch the fireflies. I remember catching fireflies with my children and always saying that the best part was letting the fireflies go free.

I can see the outline of the girls' old swing set in the dark. Many evenings, the female red-tailed hawk will perch on the swing set's top beam. She has raised her fledgling again this year. I think of the mother hawk and myself as keeping each other company in the early evenings. But it is late and she has already roosted deeper in the woods tonight. I am glad to know she is nearby. In the mornings I often see her soaring in her wide arcs, making her high-pitched, echoing calls. How she soars!

Reading Mentioned in <u>Survival Snapshots</u>:

Bolen, Jean Shinoda, <u>Goddesses in Older Women: Archetypes in Women Over Fifty</u>. New York: HarperCollins, 2001.

Bradshaw, John, <u>Family Secrets: What You Don't Know Can Hurt You</u>. New York: Bantam, 1995.

Kushner, Harold S., <u>When Bad Things Happen to Good People</u>. New York: Schocken Books, 1981.

Made in the USA
Charleston, SC
06 March 2015